# HITLER'S WAR OF EXTINCTION

Rare German Colour Photographs from the Eastern Front

TEXT BY SIMON FORTY
IMAGES FROM IAN STEWART SPRING

Greenhill Books

## Acknowledgements (from Simon Forty)

Thanks to all those who contributed to this book, especially Ian Hughes for the design, Patrick Hook for his help with vehicle recognition and Matthew Acred for his help with the Luftwaffe captions. In particular I'd like to thank Richard Charlton Taylor for materially helping with captioning and content, and Jessica Cuthbert-Smith for editorially saving the author's blushes on more than one occasion! Most of the quotations come from Friedrich Sander's diaries as published by Greenhill and cited in the Bibliography.

## Acknowledgements (from Ian Spring)

I would like to warmly thank, for the amazing contribution of extra images and technical research information, David Williams, Akira Takiguchi, John Avis, Matthew Acred and the recently deceased Udo Wagner. Also a big thank you for a wonderful book team with Michael Leventhal and Simon Forty. Finally, from my heart, thank you to my parents Sylvia and Declan and also my amazing daughter Fiona Frances Spring for their support and love. Without them, I would not be where I am today.

*Hitler's War of Extinction: Rare German Colour Photographs from the Easterm Front*

Greenhill Books

First published in 2025
by Greenhill Books, Lionel Leventhal Ltd
c/o Pen & Sword Books Ltd,
George House, Unit 12 & 13, Beevor Street, Off Pontefract Road, Barnsley, South Yorkshire S71 1HN
For more information on our books, please visit
www.greenhillbooks.com, email contact@greenhillbooks.com
or write to us at the above address.



CIP data records for this title are available from the British Library
ISBN 978-1-80500-131-7
Typeset and designed by www.mousematdesign.com
Printed and bound in India by Replika Press Pvt. Ltd.

FSC www.fsc.org MIX Paper | Supporting responsible forestry FSC™ C016779

# Contents

# Introduction

A WAR OF EXTINCTION took place on the Eastern Front during the Second World War when two existentially opposed ideologies fought for survival. Millions of soldiers and civilians died, each side being as uncaring of their own people as their enemies. Each side also had an agenda of genocide: the Nazis against the Jews; for the Soviets it was the Poles, as had been pursued in Ukraine (over 47,000 murdered in 1937–38) and at Katyn (over 15,000 in 1939). Each side was under the thrall of a dictator whose grasp of power was total, and whose secret police cowed the populace. Each side controlled the education of its youth and had instilled a personality cult for its leader and complete belief in the tenets of his ideology.

The Eastern Front battlefield was huge, as large as any in history. It stretched some 3,500km (over 2,000 miles) from Murmansk in the Arctic north to the Caucasus mountains in the south; from the Polish border 1,000km (600 miles) to the outskirts of Moscow. The different environments and the varieties of weather created a considerable strain on the German procurement and logistics systems.

On duty and suitably wrapped for a harsh environment, this soldier (below) patrols the northern tip of Europe. Towards the end of 1944 the Finnish surrender and Soviet advances pushed the German Army back into Norway. Operation *Birke* allowed an effective retreat to the prepared *Sturmbock* positions. Winter set in and it was 27 April 1945 before the last Germans quit Finland.

The most southerly extent of German control was 90km (55 miles) from Grozny, the capital of today's Chechnya and one of the key objectives of 1942's *Fall Blau*. During the Battle of Stalingrad, afraid of being cut off by Soviet advances, HG B withdrew to the Kuban bridgehead. They never returned, and the oilfields – and a potential thrust into the Middle East – failed to materialise.

Here, the spoils of free time (*inset*), somewhere in Caucasus – a small pike supplements the rations. All armies live off the land to some extent, particularly in static positions

Behind the fighting troops came the Einsatzgruppen. The Nazis' genocidal ambitions lost them any chance of winning the support of the local populations – although this is not to say that initially there were no collaborators. Many were pleased to have lost the Soviet yoke. They were happy to be able to reinstate the religious and social customs that had been suppressed since the Russian Revolution. Strong nationalist views existed in many countries. Quickly, however, German shortsightedness and barbarity played into the Soviet partisans' hands.

The Germans had no intention of winning over the population they conquered; they simply wanted to exploit it. But there were cracks they could have used. The link, for example, between the partisans and locals was often strained. Many areas, low on food and affected by the fighting, had difficult relationships with partisans who came to them by night and took food and men to fight. On top of this, not all Soviet troops joined partisan groups. Many PoWs chose to help the German Army in order to ensure themselves a supply of rations and a slightly better chance of survival. It is interesting to note that one of the main reasons for the Soviet High Command's interest in and assistance for partisan units was that it helped maintain Communist Party influence in the occupied areas. Indeed, for some time Stalin was concerned about arming partisans whom he might later have to disarm forcibly.

Here, an Einsatzgruppe unit forces Soviet prisoners to dig a grave – possibly for themselves.

Nazis and Soviets had been uneasy bedfellows from the 1920s, when partnership served their purposes. Both countries had been weakened by their losses in the First World War. Germany struggled to come to terms with its defeat and the overthrow of the Kaiser. In Russia, having just won a bloody civil war, the new Soviet government needed stability from external menace to develop its internal agendas. So, the Soviets provided Germany with secret locations where the German armed forces could rebuild in repudiation of the 1919 Versailles Treaty. This stopped as soon as the Nazis came to power in 1933. However, after six years of mutual abuse, they became co-conspirators in 1939, first with a non-aggression pact and then with the dismemberment of Poland.

In spite of this political rapprochement, both the Nazis and the Soviet communists had ensured their people knew who their real enemies were. Hitler had on many occasions promoted anti-Slavism, then conflated his hatred of communism and Jews into an international 'Jewish-Bolshevik' conspiracy that could only be ended by the subjugation – and, at first tacitly, the extermination – of Jews and commissars. The oppression of the Jews started in 1933. It reached its first crescendo on Kristallnacht, 9–10 November 1938. After this, 30,000 male Jews were sent to the concentration camps (Dachau opened in 1933; Sachsenhausen in 1936 and

Buchenwald in 1937). On 30 January 1939 Hitler talked about '*die Vernichtung der Jüdischen Rasse in Europa*' – the extermination of the Jewish race in Europe – in the Reichstag.

The extermination proper started in Poland. In September 1939, just before the invasion of the country, Hitler said: 'My Death's Head Units [*Totenkopfverbände*] stand ready under orders to mercilessly send to death without pity or mercy all men, women, and children of Polish descent or language.'[1]

The annihilation of the Jews was not the only reason the Nazis struck east. Hitler had been vocal in promoting the idea of the need for Aryan Lebensraum there, with the Slavs either obliterated or enslaved. *Mein Kampf* outlines these ideas and plans. Hitler restated them in a military meeting on 30 March 1941 on the eve of Operation *Barbarossa*, the German invasion of the Soviet Union, as recorded in notes by Generaloberst Franz Halder, Chief of the General Staff of the Oberkommando des Heeres (OKH – High Command of the Army):

Both Germany and the Soviet Union were one-party states with various state enforcement agencies. Lenin's were the Cheka; his successor Stalin's the NKVD, who carried out the Great Purges of the 1930s. Hitler and the Nazis also had their share of bully-boys. The SA (Sturmabteilung or storm troopers) was the paramilitary arm the Nazi Party raised for protection. It played a significant part in Hitler's rise but the increasing power and ambition of the Brownshirts became a threat. The Night of the Long Knives of 1934 put an end to that! Note the SA unit insignia patch at top left on the flags, seen here during a SA sports day in 1939.

Germany and the Soviet Union made great use of propaganda to convince their populations of the regime's legitimacy and infallibility, particularly aiming this propaganda at young people. The Hitlerjugend (HJ – Hitler Youth) was a male paramilitary organisation that indoctrinated 14–18-year-olds with myths of Aryan racial superiority to ensure the future of Nazi Germany. Once the Nazis took power, they amalgamated all other groups into the HJ and membership became compulsory so that by 1939 it had topped 7.25 million. Most of the activities resembled military training, including weapon familiarisation and basic fighting tactics. In the photo can be seen the HJ fanfare trumpet banners with the unusual black on white and more usual white on black single *sigrunes* (Old Norse victory rune), the emblem of the junior boys of the HJ. From Hitlerjugend to Reichsarbeitsdienst (RAD – Reich Labour Service) to Wehrmacht was the path of many German boys.

Our goals in Russia: Crush armed forces, break up state.

Clash of two ideologies. Crushing denunciation of Bolshevism, identified with a social criminality. Communism is an enormous danger for our future. We must forget the concept of comradeship between soldiers. A Communist is no comrade before nor after the battle. This is a war of extermination. If we do not grasp this, we shall still beat the enemy, but 30 years later we shall again have to fight the Communist foe. We do not wage war to preserve the enemy.

War against Russia: Extermination of the Bolshevist Commissars and of the Communist intelligentsia. The new states must be Socialist, but without intellectual classes of their own. Groups of a new intellectual class must be prevented. A primitive Socialist intelligentsia is all that is needed. We must fight against the poison of disintegration. This is no job for military courts. The individual troop commanders must know the issues at stake. They must be leaders in this fight. The troops must fight back with the methods with which they are attacked. Commissars and GPU men are criminals and must be dealt with as such. This need not mean that the troops should get out of hand. Rather, the commander must give orders which express the common feelings of his men.

This war will be very different from the war in the West. In the East, harshness today means lenience in the future. Commanders must make the sacrifice of overcoming their personal scruples.[2]

It was not just boys who were involved, as this Nazi sports day shows. Gymnastics played an important role – these girls sport the emblem of the Deutsche Arbeitsfront (German Labour Front) which had taken the place of trades unions in the Nazi state. There were various female organisations, including the Bund Deutscher Mädel (German Girls League) and the NS Frauenschaft (Nazi Women's League). Although Hitler promoted the idea of a woman's place being at home having children, he accepted that nurses were essential. Later on, as it became necessary, women became involved in industry and the armed forces – Wehrmachtshelferin (armed forces' female helpers) – nicknamed *Blitzmädel*. This allowed more men to be sent to the front to replenish the ranks.

Hitler's views on commissars were put into orders on 12 May 1941, five weeks before the invasion of the Soviet Union, as the Nuremberg Tribunal's judgment on the head of the Oberkommando der Wehrmacht (OKW – High Command of the Wehrmacht), Generalfeldmarschall Wilhelm Keitel made clear:

> … the OKW urged upon Hitler a directive of the OKH that political commissars be liquidated by the Army. Keitel admitted the directive was passed on to field commanders. And on 13th May Keitel signed an order that civilians suspected of offences against troops should be shot without trial, and that prosecution of German soldiers for offences against civilians was unnecessary. On 27th July all copies of this directive were ordered destroyed without affecting its validity. Four days previously he signed another order that legal punishment was inadequate and troops should use terrorism.[3]

Both the leadership and the population of the Soviet Union were aware of the threat from Nazism. In 1936 Germany and Russia had been involved on opposite sides in the Spanish Civil War. While German technical assistance to Franco's Nationalists proved more effective than the Soviets' to the Republicans, the hardware had mixed results. The tanks (mainly PzKpfw Is) were no match for the larger numbers of Soviet armoured vehicles (mainly T-26s and BT-5s), but the power of the 8.8cm Flak guns used in an anti-tank role more than made up for this. Soviet assistance certainly postponed the Republicans' defeat, but it was never enough to give them any real hope of victory.

The ideological opposition of the two countries meant it came as a shock to the rest of the world when they signed a non-aggression pact in 1939. It was strictly political. When German Minister of Foreign Affairs Joachim von Ribbentrop suggested that the agreement should include a statement about Russo-German friendship, Stalin said: 'The Soviet Government cannot suddenly present to the nation assurances of friendship when the National Socialist Government has been slinging mud at it for six years.'

The Soviet rationale for the pact was straightforward: the USSR felt let down by the western powers who had done little to contain Hitler's expansionist policies. Stalin did not want to fight Germany without allies. He wanted to have time to deal with Japanese incursions in the far east of the USSR and more time to prepare for the war he expected in the west.

However, war came more quickly than he anticipated. Immediately, as a result of the German invasion of Poland on 5 September 1939, he removed a million skilled workers from their factories in a partial call-up, in spite of the inevitable production shortfall that would result the next year. After taking control of eastern Poland, Stalin also took the opportunity to start a murderous pogrom of captured Polish intelligentsia and military personnel.

Both countries' leaders have gone down in history as evil, inhumanly cruel dictators who cared little for their people. Hitler, especially towards the end, wanted to leave nothing remaining in Germany for any who survived the final battles. As a military leader, the success of his armies led him to overvalue his own – and their – abilities. His meddling with tactical matters and lack of strategic insights condemned Germans to their fate, although most went to their ends believing in his genius.

Stalin – seen here on a propaganda poster found in Ukraine in 1942 (Lenin is on the left) – had already proved he was quite happy to let the kulaks, Ukrainians, Soviet intelligentsia and other political prisoners die in their thousands. As a wartime leader he was as ruthless and arbitrary as Hitler, but he learned he had to leave his generals to operate by themselves, allowing them sufficient space to learn on the job.

Stalin wanted a defensive buffer between the USSR and Germany, and Finnish territory and Baltic ports were part of that requirement. When the Finns refused to hand over their land, the Soviet Union attacked. The results, initially, were disastrous as the smaller Finnish Army humiliated the Soviets. The world in general – and the Germans in particular – took note of Soviet deficiencies. They would have been well advised to look closely at what followed, as Stalin ruthlessly executed scapegoats, rearranged his forces' command structure and attacked again, this time with deadly efficiency – and at great cost to his own forces – in spite of the winter cold. Soon Finland sued for an armistice.

After the fall of Poland, Stalin forced agreements with the Baltic states of Estonia, Latvia and Lithuania to allow Soviet troop movements through and the establishment of military bases in their countries. By August 1940, all three countries had become republics in the Soviet Union and their leaders were in Siberia. Bessarabia's oilfields followed next as Stalin took them from Romania.

The Soviet Union had benefited territorially from the pact with Germany and after the Finnish debacle had also been able to identify and winnow out of its ranks some less capable senior commanders. These included Defence Commissar Marshal Kliment Voroshilov, who had survived the Great Purge and was one of Stalin's closest confidants. In spite of this, in 1941 the Soviet armed forces were in a poor condition to face the onslaught of the battle-hardened, experienced German Wehrmacht.

It had all looked so good in the mid-1930s when the Soviets led the world in the development of armoured vehicles and modern all-arms tactics. Then came the Great Purge of the armed forces in 1936–38, a result of Stalin's fear of a military coup. It particularly affected senior officers – many of the purged junior officers were rehabilitated – and this had a significant impact in 1938–41 as the Soviet armed forces saw a 250 per cent increase in personnel, from 1.5 million (1938) to just under 5.4 million on the eve of *Barbarossa*. Few officers had held their positions for more than a year when the Germans attacked. Additionally, the defence lines that had been built along the old borders from the late 1920s were set aside for new ones on the Polish border. Most of these had not been completed in June 1941.

The Soviets may have been taken by surprise by the timing of the actual *Barbarossa* attack but they had known the Germans would come. The Soviet population was also expecting it – and confidently expecting to repel it. They believed in their leaders and their cause. Throughout the 1930s, Soviet propaganda – posters, films, written media – had been full of patriotic stories, many about the heroes of the past such as Alexander Nevsky, Alexander Suvorov and, of course, the architect of Napoleon's defeat, Mikhail Kutuzov. The young were particularly committed to the communist message and believed that any invader would fail. They and the Soviet military thought they would be able to slow or hold any attack, allowing time for full mobilisation and then a comprehensive victory.

It did not play out like that. The Soviet leadership had had fair warning of the tactical issues. The Soviet expectation was that the primary axis of an attack would be towards Ukraine – partly because Stalin thought the Germans would head for the USSR's fertile breadbasket. In the Moscow war games of December 1940 Marshal Georgy Zhukov played out a successful enemy invasion of the USSR, exposing the defensive frailties of this plan and teaching a salutary lesson.

## Operation *Barbarossa*

Stalin had hoped that by not mobilising he would not provoke Germany, but he did begin a number of defensive procedures. David Glantz and Jonathan House suggest that the Soviets were 'creeping up to war',[4] citing the forces moving to the border districts in the west from the Trans-Baikal, Ural and Siberian military districts between 26 April and 10 May 1941. Further, on 13 May twenty-eight rifle divisions and four army HQs were ordered to the border – this movement was still in its early stages when the Germans attacked – and in early June the general staff called up 800,000 reservists.

As we know, the Soviet preparations did not work. On 22 June 1941 – only two days before the 129th anniversary of Napoleon's invasion – Operation *Barbarossa* started. The Germans swept all before them. Hitler, the German general staff and most outside observers expected a swift Blitzkrieg, but few of them could have predicted what actually happened. Halder was almost euphoric:[5]

> On the whole, then, it may be said even now that the objective to shatter the bulk of the Russian Army this side of the Dvina and Dniepr, has been accomplished. ... It is thus probably no overstatement to say that the Russian Campaign has been won in the space of two weeks. Of course, this does not yet mean that it is closed. The sheer geographical vastness of the country and the stubbornness of the resistance, which is carried on with all means, will claim our efforts for many more weeks to come.

The German military training regime in the prewar years was excellent and ensured the troops went into battle with a keen sense of what they needed to do. That it worked well was evinced by the Blitzkrieg campaigns – and in turn the 1939–41 experience was invaluable for *Barbarossa*. Around sixty Panzers took part in the invasion of Norway in April–June 1940 as part of Panzer-Abteilung 40: thirty PzKpfw Is, fifteen PzKpfw IIs, between seven and ten PzKpfw IIIs, three PzKpfw NbFz VIs and five kleiner Panzerbefehlswagen (PzBefWg) I command tanks, one of which heads this column (above left). The unit transferred to Finland in winter 1942/43 and became part of 25. Panzer-Division.

The Blitzkrieg in France saw larger forces involved than in Norway but the result was the same: a huge German triumph. By the time *Barbarossa* was launched, the Wehrmacht thought itself invincible. This SdKfz 10 halftrack (above right) could carry two crew and up to six passengers and was usually used as a prime mover for light artillery pieces. Its bench seats made it an excellent dormitory. Note the canvas top and sides.

He went on rather more cautiously:

> Once we are across the Dvina and Dniepr, it will be less a question of smashing enemy armies, than of denying the enemy possession of his production centres and so prevent his raising a new army with the aid of his gigantic industrial potential and his inexhaustible manpower resources.

Hitler was even more optimistic. He thought his men would reach Moscow in four weeks and believed that the great defeats would see Stalin toppled by his own people. And as his armies moved east, so they were followed by the support elements that were crucial to maintain their military expansion: logistics, medical facilities, maintenance depots, and those who would provide the new civil administration. Many of these instruments of Nazi political domination were – of course – single-mindedly concerned with heinous activities that had been seen in other areas subjugated by the Nazis: genocide, looting, exploitation. As an example of the level of exterminations, Halder noted on 26 September: 'Mental institutions in sector of AGp. [ArmeeGruppe] North. Russians regard the feeble-minded as holy. Killing nevertheless necessary.'[6] And while the main proponents of this were the SS-Totenkopfverbände (SS-Death's Head Units who ran the concentration and extermination camps), Ordnungspolizei (Order Police) and Einsatzgruppen (Action Squads), they were aided and abetted from the start by the German Army.

There was little attempt to win over 'hearts and minds'. All the potential goodwill that might have been shown to the invaders in the Baltic states or Ukraine by those who longed to rid themselves of the communist yoke – including the disaffected kulaks or old White Russians – dissipated in the face of the barbarism of the Germans as they looted and exploited the conquered territories. Instead of cooperation, there was defiance.

The maltreatment of civilians was extended to Soviet PoWs. Less than three months after the start of *Barbarossa*, on 8 September, the OKW ordered camp guards: 'Escaping POWs are to be fired upon immediately without warning … Leniency, even towards the hard-working and obedient POW, is out of line.'[7]

Soviet PoWs were treated appallingly by the Germans. Certainly, there were a lot of them, and hiccups in supplies might be accepted as a wartime problem, but the Germans deliberately set the ration levels low, leading to malnutrition. Combined with lack of medical care and hard labour, it is unsurprising that dysentery and typhus set in. Of the nearly 6 million Red Army PoWs, fewer than a third survived captivity. Also unsurprising is what this led to: on the one hand, more soldiers joined partisan groups rather than surrendering; on the other, from about this time, many became Hiwis – *Hilfswilliger*, auxiliaries who helped the German Army. There were 600,000 of them by 1944. They took on the role rather than die of starvation. Once they had done so there was no going back: if they were taken by the Red Army they could expect little mercy – even PoWs were treated with suspicion. All stragglers, escaped PoWs or civilians who reached Soviet lines went to filtration camps to determine whether they were traitors or not.

Many of the Red Army soldiers behind enemy lines joined the substantial number of partisans. The threat they posed increased sufficiently for Keitel to send out the order 'Combating the Communist Uprising in the Occupied Areas [of the Soviet Union]'. The Nuremberg Tribunal reported:

> On 16th September, 1941, Keitel ordered that attacks on soldiers in the East should be met by putting to death 50 to 100 Communists for one German soldier, with the comment that human life was less than nothing in the East. On 1st October he ordered military commanders always to have hostages to execute when German soldiers were attacked.[8]

A ghastly example of this sort of reprisal was perpetrated in Kiev (today's Kyiv) on 29–30 September. Timed demolition charges and mines left by retreating Soviet troops created explosions that killed many German soldiers and formed the pretext for the infamous massacre of innocents at Babi Yar by elements of Einsatzgruppe C. Over 33,000 Jews were shot, most of them women, children and elderly people.

Equally horrific was the murder of thousands of political prisoners by the Soviet People's Commissariat for Internal Affairs (NKVD) as they retreated in the face of the German invasion. It is difficult to put figures on the NKVD atrocities that took place in Poland, Belarus, the Baltic states, Ukraine and Russia itself, but well over 100,000 people were murdered. The killings continued as the fighting extended. The Soviets held off the German assaults in 1941–42 not just through courage and self-sacrifice but also through fear, as progressively ruthless orders came from the top of the chain of command. First, NKVD blocking detachments were ordered to detain deserters with ruthless reprisals. A report to Lavrentiy Beria, head of the NKVD, said that between 22 June and 10 October the detachments detained 657,364 military personnel and shot 10,201 of them. Order No. 270 of 16 August 1941 outlined that commanders and political officers who deserted or surrendered were to be considered malicious and shot on sight. Their families would be arrested and deprived of public benefits and assistance. It emphasised that

On the Eastern Front both the Germans and the Soviets executed those they thought were cowards. Indeed, execution could be the result of the most minor misdemeanour. In this case, we probably witness a reprisal after an incident. Note among the onlookers the policeman on the left (identified by his cap badge), the Hiwi auxiliary volunteer with the flat cap and dark coat and an assorted group of German soldiers.

encircled units should fight to the last. The trouble was that the order led to excessive violence as officers often executed stragglers to ensure that they themselves were not killed. On 4 October Order No. 391 tried to curb these excesses.

Order No. 227 of 28 July 1942 resulted from the losses in the south after *Fall Blau*. The order increased the number of penal battalions (*shtrafbaty*) and companies (*shtrafroty*). It also increased army blocking detachments. Between 1 August and 5 October 1942, these detained 140,755 people, of whom 1,189 were shot. However, as the tide turned after Stalingrad, the blocking detachments had less work to do and on 29 October 1944, by Order No. 349, Stalin disbanded them.

The Germans also had penal battalions – Strafbataillone – administered by the Feldgendarmerie (later by the Feldjägerkorps set up in September 1943). They were forced to undertake suicidal missions, but those who survived were allowed to rejoin ordinary units. By the end of the war, 50,000 had served in these battalions.

The Germans too were prepared to execute their own men: 22,500 were sentenced to death for desertion (at least 15,000 were executed). Many others (23,000–50,000) died after being found guilty of insubordination, defeatism or bad-mouthing the Führer. Similar to the Soviet attacks on the families of the guilty, the Germans invoked *Sippenhaft* – kin liability, the worst examples of which followed the 20 July 1944 bomb plot.

## *Rasputitsa* and Winter

For the armies fighting in the war of extinction on the Eastern Front, there was an additional threat to that posed by the enemy: the Russian weather. First, there was the *rasputitsa*, the autumn and spring rainy seasons that glued down mechanised troops in a morass of mud. This held up the German assault on Moscow in 1941. Then there was the Russian winter. Just as Napoleon's army had succumbed to the cold, so the German Army froze during that first winter. With Moscow in sight, on 4–5 December Guderian had to sound the retreat as temperatures dropped below -60°F. Part of the problem was organisational: the cold-weather clothing and equipment were in depots awaiting shipping to the front, but because of logistical problems they had not been sent. Arrogantly, the invaders had assumed it would all be over by Christmas – and that their to-date excellent logistics would be able to cope.

It wasn't and they didn't. The huge distances involved and the attrition to German powered transport caused by the terrain and lack of metalled roads were compounded by the German Army's reliance on horses and railways. The German horses could not cope with the cold – unlike the Russian ponies – and the Germans could not make the railways work well enough. The Soviets had destroyed as much infrastructure as they could when they retreated and had taken much of the motive power and rolling stock along with them. To use their own equipment, the Germans had to rebuild the lines to their gauge. They accomplished this, often with remarkable speed, but there were never sufficient lines and they never operated smoothly. Overlapping jurisdictions, the overriding need for supplies for the troops, partisan demolitions – to read through Halder's diaries is to read a litany of logistical problems. By the time 6. Armee reached Stalingrad, for example, it was receiving four supply trains a day on average, when it realistically needed between eight and ten.[9]

Between 1938 and 1939 the German Army mobilised at least 400,000 horses. This number was increased by those taken at the Anschluss and then from Czechoslovakia and Poland. In 1940, Holland, Belgium and France yielded heavier breeds, better for artillery. By exploiting the conquered countries, in June 1941 the Germans had assembled 625,000 horses. All would be needed. Indeed, it is estimated that the German Army used about 2.75 million horses during the war. Naturally, staggering numbers were killed – and not just from the fighting. Thousands were 'meals on legs' as circumstances dictated. Here, a Red Cross wagon's motive power lies dead in an unknown village in eastern Europe.

The result was huge in terms of human – and equine – suffering as frostbite and other cold injuries decimated the German ranks. This contributed to the success of the Soviet counteroffensive around Moscow, the first major defeat the Germans suffered against the Soviets. By this time, the Germans were exhausted, with manpower levels dipping and hardware suffering from the wear and tear of six months' fighting. They had been happily surprised by the ease with which the campaign had opened; now they were hanging on for dear life, amazed at the seemingly limitless depths of the Soviet manpower pool. The Germans may have taken huge numbers of prisoners, but the Soviet forces still had not folded in the same way that the troops in the west had done. They had fought on, trading men and materiel for time, time that allowed more troops to be rushed to the front. At Smolensk, Bryansk and Vyazma, crushing pockets of resistance had taken longer than expected, and the cost was rising. The time bought by the sacrifice of the Red Army troops in these pockets allowed Zhukov to build Moscow's defences and prepare reserves for the counterattack, which pushed the Germans back.

What the Soviet winter counterattack did not do was relieve Leningrad, besieged by the Germans since 8 September. Deliberately allowing the civilians to starve, bombarding the city by day and night, the Germans maintained the siege for 900 days. Over 1.5 million Soviets – the vast majority civilians – died, many of starvation, in the siege before it was relieved in 1944.

## *Fall Blau*

At the start of 1942 German forces were in dire need of reinforcement. Heeresgruppe Mitte (HG Mitte), for example, had suffered 111,944 killed, wounded and missing in the last two months of 1941. German tank losses in the year June 1941 to June 1942 were 4,667.[10] However, by June 1942 nearly 5,000 new tanks had been built. New equipment and replacement troops were provided for the next major German thrust: *Fall Blau*, towards the Caucasus and its oilfields.

Oil was always a crucial commodity for the German war machine and the Caucasus could supply exactly what it needed. The ranks of Heeresgruppen Nord and Mitte were reduced to give Heeresgruppe Süd the men and tanks it needed: in total, it had a force of around 1.5 million men (1.2 million German, the others Romanian, Hungarian, Italian and Slovak), nearly 2,000 tanks and 1,700 aircraft. Opposing them were 1.7 million Soviet troops with 3,000 tanks in situ and, after the attack happened, large numbers of reinforcements.

*Fall Blau* started on 28 June 1942 and quickly made headway – so much so that Stalin issued Order No. 227: Not one step back! It made no difference. The Germans continued to advance and although their losses were heavy, they were a lot less than the Soviets'. When the Germans took Rostov, Hitler changed HG Süd's orders, dividing it into two. The

As the new year of 1942 was rung in, Germany was still basking in the pleasure of swift victories. There had been casualties, but victory in the east was very close. While some may have harboured doubts, the success of the Nazis' political ambitions was plain to see. Germany ruled Europe. It had recovered and extended its borders. Its Wehrmacht had proved unbeatable. Civil disorder was a thing of the past. The communist Soviet Union would fall soon and then peace would come and the boys would return home. Little did they know that 1942 was the year of change. Germans would not feel quite as safe in their homes as the RAF's bombing campaign – soon to be joined by the USAAF – got underway.

Germans also needed to redistribute their forces to combat Soviet attacks elsewhere. HG Süd lost eleven divisions (including four Panzer and motorised divisions). These were replaced by seven allied divisions (three Italian, four Romanian) with eight more Romanian divisions in September.

By early November the southern thrust – HG A – had advanced over 1,000km (600 miles) and was tantalisingly close to the oilfields; the northern – HG B – had taken 90 per cent of Stalingrad on the Volga. There the assault faltered. Overextended supply lines, critical fuel shortages, exposed flanks, significant casualties and a determined defence brought the attack to a halt. And then things got a whole lot worse. On 19 November the Red Army surprised the Germans with a powerful attack – Operation *Uranus* – that crushed the Germans' allies (mainly Romanian Third and Fourth Armies) protecting 6. Armee's flank and enveloped the Germans in Stalingrad. The result was a catastrophe for the Axis and a bloodbath. Over a million soldiers and civilians on both sides died in the fighting – some estimates are as high as 3 million. Nearly 300,000 troops from the German Army and its allies surrendered in early February 1943. The extended fighting at Stalingrad had given the Germans time to extract HG B from the Caucasus and retreat back to where *Fall Blau* had started. Thanks to Erich von Manstein's 'miracle' on the Chir river and retaking of Kharkov (today's Kharkiv), the German line was steadied and both sides waited for the next move. Would the Germans attack or hold steady and wait for a counterattacking opportunity?

They decided to attack the Kursk salient but, crucially, waited until July to do so. That gave time for both sides to re-equip and for the Soviet defences to prepare. The Germans needed the break. On 1 April 1943, after the huge losses at Stalingrad and the associated fighting, the Ostheer had 2.7 million men, 1,336 tanks and 6,360 guns; the Red Army 5.8 million men, more than 6,000 tanks and 20,000 guns.[11]

The German reinforcements for the Battle of Kursk included new types of tank: PzKpfw V Panthers (200 were rushed to the battlefield too early, their subsequent automotive performance was awful), PzKpfw VI Tigers (launched earlier in the year outside Leningrad with limited success) and the huge SdKfz 184 Panzerjäger Tiger (P) – the Ferdinand – which made big claims of success at Kursk: schwere Panzerjäger Abteilung 653 claimed 320 enemy tanks for the loss of only thirteen Ferdinands. The trouble was that there were only ninety-one Ferdinands (later renamed Elefant) built. They and the Panthers and Tigers epitomised the huge difference between the two sides' technology. The Germans' was often brilliant but had huge technical issues they did not have time to iron out – as many Tigers were destroyed by their own crews because of automotive problems or lack of fuel (the Tiger could only manage some 80km (50 miles) cross-country on its internal fuel supply) than were killed by the enemy. They could never mass-produce the third-generation tanks in sufficient numbers to make anything more than a local impact.

On the other hand, the Soviet technology was predicated on mass-production, usability and rugged construction. And they had a lot of vehicles: if one was hit, another took its place. The Germans had no such depth of materiel and expended great effort in bringing knocked-out vehicles back into the service – one reason for the huge disparity between German and Soviet tank loss figures.

On 22 May 1939 Italian Fascist leader Benito Mussolini and Hitler signed the Pact of Steel, a military alliance that led to German involvement in North Africa and the Balkans. The Regia Marina (Italian Navy) was well armed – although it lacked radar – and performed with mixed results, mainly in the Mediterranean, with some assets seeing action in the Black Sea campaign and on Lake Ladoga. The Regia Aeronautica Italiana (Italian Air Force) had helped transport Franco's Army of Africa to Spain and had performed excellently in the Spanish Civil War, but its aircraft were outdated and the Corpo Aereo Spedizione (Italian Air Force Expeditionary Corps) in Russia was initially only 100 or so aircraft strong. The Italian Army contribution to *Barbarossa* was also surprisingly small at first – the Corpo di Spedizione Italiano in Russia (CSIR – Italian Expeditionary Force in Russia) was around 62,000 men strong – and arrived in theatre in mid-July 1941. Mussolini increased its size considerably in 1942 when the CSIR became part of the 235,000-strong Armata Italiana in Russia (ARMIR – Italian Army in Russia), destroyed at Stalingrad and withdrawn in 1943. One thing, however, is certain: the Italian armed forces were immensely brave and withstood awful conditions with poor clothing and equipment and were certainly undervalued by their ally. Nowhere is that bravery better shown than in the cavalry component of the CSIR. On 24 August 1942, with an Italian unification cry from the nineteenth century on their lips, the Savoia Cavelleria successfully charged Russian lines at Izbushensky, one of the last major cavalry charges in history.

A Royal Hungarian Army sergeant wearing a *bocskai* side cap with national cockade and the red arm of service triangle denoting artillery. Note the sergeant's collar badge of rank. The Hungarians on the Eastern Front – Second Army – lacked transport, armour and air assets. They spent a year at the front after moving up in June 1942. Short of training, food and cold-weather clothing, the army was destroyed during the Battle of Stalingrad while defending German 6. Armee's flank against Soviet Operations *Uranus* and *Little Saturn*. Of the 200,000 who started out, only 40,000 returned to Hungary, with over 50,000 taken prisoner. Needless to say, the German Army did not think much of them.

Romanian troops on the Eastern Front outnumbered all the other German allies combined – over a million men by summer 1944. They had good reason for their involvement: to regain the territories they had lost to the Soviet Union (Bessarabia and northern Bukovina) and Hungary (northern Transylvania). They picked up the former quickly after *Barbarossa* started. They accepted a deal with Hitler and were promised Transnistria in place of Transylvania but were not able to take over that area before the Red Army took away the opportunity. The Romanian Army was heavily involved at Stalingrad, but on 23 August 1944 King Michael I staged a coup, joined the side of the Allies, and Romanian troops began fighting their erstwhile allies, sustaining casualties of around 165,000. As a result, the Treaty of Paris in 1947 restored Transylvania, although Romania lost territories to Bulgaria and the Soviet Union.

This Romanian soldier is wearing a Dutch-made helmet, manufactured under contract for the Romanian Army and designated Model 39. The first batches had King Carol II's cypher on the front – two Cs topped by a crown – but when he abdicated (not by choice!) in 1940 these were removed. The rifle is a Czech vz24.

Although the Nazis were initially against allowing non-Aryans to enter the armed forces – as Oleysa Kromeychuk writes, Hitler said 'only Germans should carry weapons, not Slavs, Czechs, Cossacks, or Ukrainians', as the war progressed, they became more pragmatic. By October 1944 some 800,000 Osttruppen served in the German Army, of whom around 250,000 identified as Ukrainian. Many were forced into service but others were volunteers, usually because they were nationalists.

From the Donbas area of Ukraine and Russia the fiercely anti-communist Don Cossacks (with their distinctive black *papacha* headwear) threw in their lot with the Germans and formed two Cossack divisions that from February 1945 became the XV. SS-Kosaken-Kavallerie-Korps. Primarily used to conduct anti-partisan activities and notoriously cruel, the Cossacks offered no quarter and expected none in return. Their reputation preceded them, especially when sent to north Italy. Having supported the losing side, they and their families were forcibly repatriated at the end of the war as Stalin had demanded at Yalta. Many were executed, others disappeared into the gulags until the 1953 amnesty.

The battle that ensued at Kursk was typical of the later war years. There were many German tactical successes and significant Soviet losses but strategically all the battle accomplished was to waste German men and materiel. The Soviets themselves were suffering from manpower shortages, but they proved able to field sufficient men to ensure that the opposition's tactical successes did not translate into strategic victories. Additionally, Stalin came to trust his commanders and give them freer rein in 1944 and 1945. Hitler, on the other hand, began the process of straitjacketing his generals by poking his nose into every element of the fighting, trying to impose his will on a battlefield where the Germans were losing control.

## The Long Retreat

Soviet victories at Stalingrad and in the huge tank battles at Kursk in July 1943 saw the strategic initiative pass to the Red Army. The Germans fell back to deeply defended prepared positions that made use of major rivers: the Dnieper, Drut and Berezina. Hitler ordered the creation of *Feste Plätze* – fortified towns – to knit the defensive line together. Could this line hold against a Red Army that had now learned how to win? Three years after the start of Operation *Barbarossa*, a few days after the Normandy landings opened a new front in the west, on 22 June 1944 the Red Army unleashed Operation *Bagration*.

Hitler and Himmler visit mines in the Leoben area after the Anschluss. The key assets that Austria afforded were manpower, money and raw materials: magnesium and iron in particular. Nazi Germany's lack of raw materials and oil played an important role in deciding strategic goals. Hitler's territorial expansion started with Austria and continued in 1938 to Czechoslovakia, whose western, Czech, elements were almost surrounded by Germany after the Anschluss.

The amount of booty the Germans won in the Blitzkrieg battles of the early war years meant that German manufacturing did not need to move fully onto a proper war footing until 1944, when it produced more weapons than ever before (helped by slave labour). The conquered lands were secured after the military headed further forward and agencies loosely connected to Göring's Four-Year Plan moved in to exploit the captured territory. Taking over French, Czech and other manufacturing facilities filled an important gap in German production.

Captured weapons too were used when the occasion arose, for as long as there were spares available. These dusty infantrymen are posing with a captured T-26 tank. Based on the British Vickers 6-ton, Mark E, over 11,000 were produced from 1931 to 1941, in over fifty versions.

Within two months of the start of *Bagration*, Heeresgruppe Mitte was shattered, and the German defensive line destroyed. Clever subterfuge ensured almost complete tactical surprise. The Germans lost some half a million men killed, missing or wounded and the Soviet front line advanced to Warsaw and the Vistula. The Germans' last major base on Russian soil at Minsk fell on 3 July. Compounded by the losses that accompanied Anglo-American success in the west, the German Army had lost more men and materiel than it could cope with, this in spite of the remarkable productivity of German industry in 1944.

Too late, German industry – even though it and the rail system were pounded day and night by the Allied air forces – had turned the tap up fully and the leap in manufacturing totals was huge. In 1943 Germany had built 11,601 armoured fighting vehicles (AFVs); in 1944 18,956 – over 60 per cent more. Aircraft production soared from 20,599 all told to 35,067 – 70 per cent more, the majority fighters and ground-attack aircraft. While Albert Speer claimed the credit, partly by retaining key workers who would otherwise have been pushed into the Wehrmacht, some of this growth was simply down to the fact that German

This captured, whitewashed T-34/76 is seen in winter 1941. Note the felt and leather winter boots and the newly whitewashed helmets hanging from belts of the men of Infanterie-Regiment 470 inspecting the Soviet tank. The T-34 typifies the qualitative differences between the Germans and the Soviets. A shock to the Germans when they first encountered it, the response was the Panther, rushed into battle at Kursk. Seemingly a magnificent machine, in fact the Panther suffered from debilitating teething problems, and it took some time to work out the solutions. The T-34, on the other hand, was functional, reliable and produced in big quantities. It was not as survivable – it was underarmoured compared to German tanks – and its gun may not (certainly in the /76 version) have been as good, but there were a lot of them. As with the USA and the M4 Sherman, the Soviets went for quantity (84,000 T-34s built; as a comparison, 49,000 Shermans and 6,000 Panthers) of sturdy reliable tanks.

industry had learned through experience. The companies had slimmed down the systems and concentrated on making fewer types more quickly and cheaply. The Wehrmacht had been able to bolster its arsenal in the early part of the war with armaments taken from defeated nations. In 1943 and 1944 the industrial resources in those nations were also utilised to increase production. This extra production ensured that the losses at the front could be, in part, made up for. As a comparison, it is worth looking at Soviet tank production. In 1943 the Soviets built 15,710 T-34s alone; in 1944, 7,155 light, 17,067 medium and 4,764 heavy AFVs – nearly 29,000 vehicles, 50 per cent more than the Germans.

In spite of being lower than Soviet output, this extra German productivity made a difference. In the west Hitler was able to gamble on the Ardennes counterattack. In the east, the Panzers tried to keep Hungary and Budapest German with the three *Konrad* operations, although in the end it was clutching at straws. The Germans still had some tactical successes – but these were increasingly less common as the Allies gained experience and confidence and the German training programmes were reduced in effectiveness and duration.

The last rites on the Eastern Front started on 12 January 1945 when the Soviet assault across the Vistula started. By 2 February Soviet forces had reached the Oder, under 160km (100 miles) from Berlin. As they did so, they uncovered the shocking reality of the Holocaust – the concentration and extermination camps in Poland such as Majdanek and Auschwitz. Many of the camps had been cleared of those who could walk. They were forced – along with Allied PoWs – into death marches west. The guards tried to hide the evidence, as they had at Babi Yar when they realised they were leaving Ukraine. Try as they would, the damning evidence was plain to see, and the world was shocked at the depravities exposed. Also moving west were many of the Germans who had either lived in the east before the war or who had moved in as the population was ethnically cleansed.

The Soviet war machine paused on the Oder–Neisse line to clear Silesia and Pomerania before attacking over the Seelow Heights on 16 April. Berlin fell on 2 May 1945 and on 8–9 May other German troops surrendered. The Red Army by this time had much of eastern Europe under its control.

The war of extinction was over but the deaths and suffering would continue for many years. German PoWs were held in Soviet prison camps well into the 1950s; many of the prisoners of eastern European stock in Allied hands – those who had been fighting or coerced into fighting on the Nazi side – were handed back to the Soviets, with dire results. Germany and Austria were divided up and ruled by the victorious Allies. Those who had been involved in crimes against humanity were tried at Nuremberg – although rather fewer than might have been expected or deserved. In the Soviet Union, whose military and civilian population had suffered over 20 million deaths, there was less clemency.

Between 22 June 1941 and 20 September 1945 the Soviet Union received massive Lend–Lease aid from the western Allies: more than $50,000 million-worth from the United States and $1,300 million from the British (these are the values at the time). This included over 8,000 tanks, 427,000 of the Soviets' 665,000 trucks, as well as innumerable quantities of petroleum products, machine tools, raw materials and desperately needed foodstuffs. This is a Canadian Ford 15cwt truck that was captured by the Germans and used as a command vehicle.

## The Photographs

This book portrays the terrible events on the Eastern Front through the medium of contemporary colour photographs taken by German *Kriegsberichter* (war reporters) and soldiers at the time – a mixture of professional and amateur shots. It presents a graphic view of the battlefield and the death and destruction the war left behind. It has been made possible by the remarkable Pixpast Archive collection amassed by Ian Spring, which has already provided material for the first book on the Eastern Front and a subsequent title covering the Afrika Korps. To minimise overlap, this volume has a slightly wider brief than the first, looking at how the German Home Front contributed and taking the story through to the end of the war.

Time and storage conditions can have a bad effect on old images – particularly colour film – and Ian Spring has worked wonders to restore the images to as close a colour match as can be achieved. They provide a unique view and lasting record of the Eastern Front during the war of extinction that blighted so many lives.

German Luftwaffe reporter and photographer Otto Vieth of *Der Adler* in Russia, summer 1942, with his Leica III camera. If he uses the long lens in his right hand he will need to add a different rangefinder. A fortnightly magazine, *Der Adler* was published from 1939 to 1945 with support of the Luftwaffe. The army equivalent was *Signal*, which was published into 1945, at one time having a circulation of 2.5 million.

### Notes

[1] Romaniuk.
[2] Halder, Vol. VI, pp. 41–3.
[3] Nuremberg Tribunal, 'Judgement: Keitel'.
[4] Glantz and House.
[5] Halder, Vol. VI, p. 195.
[6] Halder, Vol. VII, p. 124.
[7] Ehrenhain Zeithain.
[8] Nuremberg Tribunal, 'Judgement: Keitel'.
[9] Liedtke, p. 373.
[10] Liedtke, Table 4.13.
[11] Figures from Glantz and House.

# 1 The German Home Front

HITLER HAD BEEN CHANCELLOR for six years when the Wehrmacht entered Poland; eight by the start of Operation *Barbarossa*. Most Germans in 1941 would have been pleased with what the Nazis had achieved during that period. They had restored Germany to its old borders – increased them even, with the Anschluss, the entry into the Sudetenland and the occupation of much of western Europe and Poland. The economy had improved too, thanks to deficit spending on infrastructure projects – many set up by the Weimar Republic but for which the Nazis took credit. Take-home pay had increased, although much of this was down to the longer working hours enabled by stifling the trades unions. This had also ensured a significant reduction in unemployment that was furthered by a huge increase in the manufacture of armaments, which rose to a peak of 75 per cent of national income by 1944.

Of course, by then 25 per cent of the workforce was slave labour: the Nazis had always intended to defray their expenses by exploiting the countries they subjugated. Much like the Roman Empire, Nazi economics were based on the booty and the slaves that they could bring home by their prowess on the battlefield. They raided the coffers of those countries, took the raw materials and manufactured goods, and indentured their population as workers for the Reich.

On the home front, there was little opposition. Most of those likeliest to cause a problem had been silenced during the Night of the Long Knives (30 June–2 July 1934) or by sending them to concentration camps. Cowed into acceptance by the unregulated activities of the Gestapo, most Germans were happy to keep their heads down and enjoy the benefits of victory. There were few sticking points; one proved to be the objections – mainly voiced by the Catholics, whose numbers had swelled thanks to the arrival of the Czechs and Austrians into Greater Germany – to the extermination of the mentally ill and physically disabled. By the time Hitler ordered it to stop, in mid-1941, that death toll had reached 70,000.

Confidence in the regime, and its likely success against communism in the east, was at its high point in early 1942. Then came the RAF's long-range attack on Lübeck on 28 March 1942. Some 300 died, but over 25,000 homes were destroyed. The attack on Cologne – Operation *Millennium* – on 30/31 May was even bigger: the first of the 1,000-bomber raids. Only 500 dead, but 45,000 buildings destroyed and damaged.

Gradually, the intensity of the war would creep into every German's life through the bombing, the mounting death toll in the east and the shortages. Hitler knew only too well the impact that shortages had had on morale during the First World War and did as much as he could to mitigate it, but after the fall of Stalingrad, the invasions of Sicily and Italy and then France, all the Germans could do was hope that their enemies' retribution would be less awful than they themselves had meted out.

## Friedrich Sander

Oberleutnant Friedrich Wilhelm Sander recorded his experiences in training and on the Eastern Front first-hand in his diary. Well written and keenly descriptive, Sander's journal provides a warts-and-all commentary on his life in Panzer-Regiment 11 between 1938, when he trained to become a member of the Panzerwaffe, to when the diaries end, in 1943. A member of the Nazi Party, Sander's views reflect those of a committed young German of the time and add a jolt of realism to our picture of the Eastern Front battles in 1941 and 1942. Starting Operation *Barbarossa* in the turret of a Czech-built PzKpfw 35(t), Sander won medals and fought with 6. Panzer-Division from the border to the gates of Moscow before wounds forced him to leave the front. The diaries ceased when he took up a position as an instructor in the combat school at Nisch in Serbia, so we know little of what he did in 1944 and 1945 other than he survived the war. The translated diary, *Blood, Dust and Snow*, was published by Greenhill Books in 2022

It was essential for morale that those at the front were reassured that all was 'normal' at home. Within reason in 1941, when *Barbarossa* began, it was – for the simple reason that the Allied bombing campaign had not begun in earnest. This typical German sitting room is almost certainly contrived, with its art deco elephant and palm tree lamp-stand on the desk with mix-and-match lampshade and wallpaper. Overlooking everything is the Führer, still in charge and still enjoying the devotion of the masses.

Of the 6 million Axis troops who lost their lives during the Second World War, over 5 million died on the Eastern Front. Unsurprisingly, this level of attrition led to manpower problems, which led to the slackening of the rules that held that only Germans could serve in the Wehrmacht. This careworn Unteroffizier is from the Munich recruiting office, as shown by his *dunkelgrün* (dark green) *Waffenfarbe* (arm of service colour) and shoulderboard insignia. From 1942 the W covered recruiting office personnel and the Roman numerals identified the *Wehrkreis*, here VII (München/Munich). His medal ribbons show he fought in the Great War. He carries (left to right) those of the Iron Cross 2nd Class (*Eisernes Kreuz 2. Klasse*), the Honour Cross of the World War 1914/1918 – with the crossed swords denoting a front-line veteran – as well as the Faithful Service Medal for twenty-five years' public service. On his breast pocket he has the SA Sports Badge in Bronze.

Some members of the Deutsches Jungvolk in der Hitlerjugend (German Youngsters in the Hitler Youth – 10–14-year-olds) having a sing-song. There is some variation in the colour of their shirts but all wear ties and toggles. They sport triangular sleeve patches denoting their district and the *sigrune* on a red circular field. As detailed in *Mein Kampf*, for the Nazis, education was less about abstruse knowledge and more about:

'training which will make him conscious of his race and a member of the folk-community'. Schooling was also planned to make sure that children were hardened physically and mentally, to prepare them for their involvement in war, to instil patriotism and, of course, devotion to the Nazi cause.

Above: German industry was slow to reach peak output. Most people thought the fighting in the east would be all over by Christmas – Sander notes in his diary in September: 'Now they have wagered a crate of beer on whether the war will be over by 20 October. Maybe we are done with it all in a month or in early November. As long as there is no snow or ice then, there is still a chance.' But the late start was also due to the slow uptake of mass-production. As Richard Overy pointed out, German mass-production was hindered by the large number of types in production, highlighting 425 different models and variants of aircraft, 151 different makes of lorry and 150 different motorcycles in production at various times during the war. Many German companies made use of forced labour and later slave labour, which often involved Jewish concentration camp workers being worked to death. Unsurprisingly, incidences of sabotage and mechanical problems proliferated.

Opposite: Friedrich Sander wrote, 'She drives a tractor and a lorry and – when needed – acts as motorcar chauffeur … When one thinks about the women at home, doing their duty in the Red Cross, in the Fluko [Flugwachkommando – aerial observation command] and in other positions – it is a joy to go to war for gals of that calibre.' On 26 June 1935 the Nazis had brought in the Reichsarbeitsdienst for all men aged between 18 and 25; they had to serve for six months of unpaid labour – increasingly often in the east after *Barbarossa* started. In 1939, when war was declared, this service was extended to women, who were mainly used for agricultural tasks, although *Arbeitsmaiden*, as Sander noted, ended up undertaking many other duties.

Above: Wounded soldiers were treated close to the battlefield and there were major hospitals in theatre, but those badly wounded or convalescing were sent home. This wounded man is seen in Leipzig, in 1941. Judging by the horizontal trouser crease at the top of his left leg, he's an amputee. If this was a war injury he would have been awarded a Wound Badge (*Verwundetenabzeichen*) in one of three classes: black for one or two wounds; silver, three or four; gold for five or more. An amputee automatically received gold. Recuperating at home was double-edged, as Friedrich Sander mentioned in his diary: 'Having spent the weekend at home with my wife and child, I now know that I have become too used to being at war. The peace and quiet at home isn't good for me, so this morning, as quickly as I could, I fled back into my hospital room. Here in the army, surrounded by my comrades, is my real home. Here I am not only tolerated, but I have an actual raison d'être: I can breathe freely again. I am free to do what I want and also manage to regain some kind of inner calm. I would like to know how many others feel as if they have lost their place at home after so many years of service or if I am just a misfit.'

Opposite: As with all armies, leave for the Wehrmacht was an escape from the reality of military life, be it from the horrors of the front line or simply no longer having to worry about the day-to-day duties required to keep the army functioning. Essential for morale even if only for a few days, this could be provided at a *Soldatenheim* (soldiers' recreation centre) or simply a location set up by a unit well behind the lines. There the soldier could take a hot shower, change clothing or delouse if the facility was available, eat better than in the field and enjoy small luxuries such as fruit, sweets and tobacco. He could catch up with the news with papers or by listening to the radio. Married soldiers had a better chance of proper authorised home leave, subject to the circumstances. And when at home, what could be better than the fun of a fair?

Leave was a chance to see the family and often to meet children born while the father was away at the front. The Nazi rise to power coincided with the breakthrough of photography as a mass cultural practice in Germany. Between 1933 and 1945 millions took photos and millions consumed images from a plethora of illustrated magazines. While this little boy in Leipzig stands in front of a field camera, it was the compact commercial 35mm Leica cameras that were usually used by soldiers. Friedrich Sander mentions film regularly in his diary: 'We also received mail … More important was a parcel with some lemons and several films which Clara had sent. In return I packed a few parcels for her, containing some films to develop and some dirty laundry.'

A Panzermann at home on leave. Much sought after, the Panzer uniform (*Panzersonderbekleidung*) was a short wrapover jacket, trousers in black with short ankle boots. The pink piping *Waffenfarbe* was discontinued in 1942. Note the lapel skull (*Totenkopf*) is the jawless Panzer version, not to be confused with the SS one, which has the jaw. The whitish 'tick' at left is on another man's uniform. Leave was important for the rehabilitation of units damaged in the fighting, but led to organisational difficulties, as there was not always enough capacity to allow it. For example, before *Fall Blau* in 1942, home leave was only possible for those who had served uninterruptedly on the Eastern Front from the start of *Barbarossa*.

High up on the ultimate leave wishlist was to go home for Christmas – with a tree, tinsel, candles and glass baubles. Christmas meant a great deal to the Germans, who had invented tree decorations like this in Thuringia in the sixteenth century. Sipping wine with his wife is a Luftwaffe Hauptmann (equivalent of RAF flight lieutenant), whose bright red collar tab is the *Waffenfarbe* colour for Flak (air defence). His medal ribbons are the First World War Iron Cross 1st Class (worn on the left breast pocket) and the Hindenburg Cross with Swords (from 1934) given to military participants of the Great War. He also has a First World War silver Wound Badge – note no swastika on it: this means it was awarded in the pre-Nazi era.

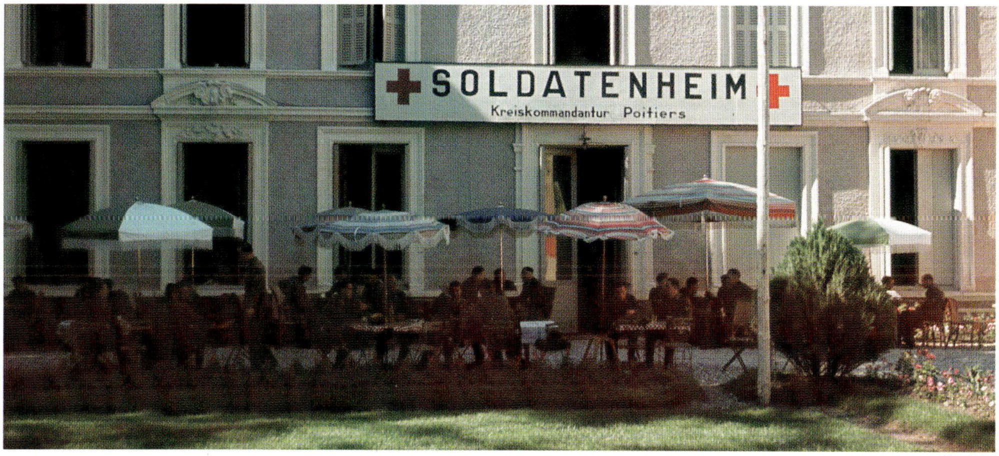


The *Soldatenheime* were run by female staff from the Deutsches Rotes Kreuz (German Red Cross). DRK-Oberfeldführerin Frieda Cleve wrote of them that every soldier, 'feels comfortable through the design of the play, reading and entertainment rooms and feels at home. He should be able to sit here when he writes home, when he wants to talk to his comrades; if he wants to read or pass the time playing games. … The soldier knows: he can go home to eat, but without having to; he can drink a glass of beer, but he can also take non-alcoholic drinks, which are particularly popular. But even without eating, he has warm, comfortable rooms, which are absolutely necessary for him, especially in the east or north.' Some soldiers' homes looked after up to 10,000 men daily and at the end of September 1942 there were 832 of them. This one is in Poitiers, France.

Das Wunschkonzert

Opposite and right: News from home is always important. War is a dislocating experience and soldiers do everything they can to maintain a connection with the people they are fighting for. That was easier to manage during the years of victory. The campaigns were short and casualties relatively light. The war changed when the Allies started bombing Germany itself (right). By this time there had been setbacks in the field. Being away from home, family and loved ones and in danger was the common lot of all soldiers, but when the Heimat was also under fire it made letters and newspapers so much more important as soldiers sought reassurance that their kin were safe.

One of the key functions of the army in Germany was to train the conscripts and reservists. The Ersatzheer (Replacement Army) had centres, and each of the divisions an HQ and training centre in its home *Wehrkreis*. This training on the 8cm Granatwerfer (GrW – mortar) 34 is at Hindenburg Barracks, Bad Kreuznach in Wehrkreis XII, where Infanterie-Regiment 107 was based. The GrW 34 was the standard German infantry mortar of the war. Over 75,000 were built along with some 74.3 million assorted rounds. Rate of fire was 15–25rpm, max range of 2.4km (1.1 miles); there were four crew members. It was a simple and effective weapon that could be broken into three man-portable loads: tube, base and frame, plus ammunition. Mortars were used heavily on the Eastern Front.

WH-40078

Above: Tank training in 1940. The vehicle is a PzKpfw I Ausf A (*Ausführung* – mark/model) *ohne Ausbau* (without turret and superstructure) used for training purposes – a Fahrschulpanzer I. Most tank driver training was undertaken by the Nationalsozialistisches Kraftfahrkorps (NSKK – Nazi Motor Corps) schools.

Opposite above: Schützen-Regiment 103 (later Panzergrenadier 103) was subordinated to 14. Panzer-Division. The unit was based in barracks at Löbau in Saxony in 1939. The *Zeltbahn* was a cleverly designed triangular tightly woven cotton gaberdine cape/poncho. When linked with three others through eye-holes and toggles, it created a four-man tent. Each man had a tent accessory bag (*Zeltzubhortasche*) that contained a 2m (6ft) rope, a four-section tent pole and two light alloy tent pegs. In combination it could sleep 8–16 men. When not in use, the *Zeltbahn* was rolled tightly with two straps and attached to the A-frame combat pack or to the Y-straps/webbing. Note the camouflage was reversible, one side darker than the other.

Opposite below: Another view of Schützen Regiment 103 training. The men wear *Drillich* – herringbone-pattern, off-white linen fatigues – which are often seen as a 'mix and match' with the standard field jacket or trousers. The motorcycle is a prewar BMW R12 750cc with sidecar. It was redesignated the R75 in 1942.

## Transport: From Reich to Russia

War is all about logistics, particularly a modern war fought at Blitzkrieg pace on many fronts. The size of the battlefields, the huge numbers of servicemen and women involved, keeping the beasts of burden – animals and machines – on the road: success was predicated on good logistics, and the key element of this was transport.

Pioneers of the internal combustion engine, automobile and *Autobahn*, in an industrialised country with an abundance of coal reserves where railways had played an important role for almost a century and were part of a pan-European net: there was every reason to assume that the Germans would be good at transport in 1941. The truth was less straightforward. The Blitzkrieg campaigns before *Barbarossa* had not needed great logistic abilities; they had not lasted for long enough. The European rail gauges were the same; for the most part the roads were metalled and good. Airfields were copious.

None of this was true in the Soviet Union. Quite simply, while Operation *Barbarossa* needed railheads for resupply and a working rail system, what it got was a logistics operation that had to rely on thousands of captured vehicles impressed into service with all the spare-parts issues that brought. The Soviet road system and the weather meant that most of these trucks were out of commission by the autumn of 1941. As the Soviets had destroyed the railway infrastructure and their loading gauge was different, the Germans had to rebuild everything. They never were able to run the number of trains necessary to supply their horse-drawn army. The problems with German rail supply in the Soviet Union are well-covered and discussed in an article by H.G.W. Davie (see Sources and Further Reading); figures in this section are from that article.

As the armoured columns penetrated ever deeper into the Soviet Union, so their supporting infantry and supply trains lagged behind. In 1941 HG Nord got to within 130km (80 miles) of Leningrad before the supply system failed. By the time it had sufficient supplies to start a major assault, it was stymied by the defences that had been set up by the Soviets in the intervening time. HG Mitte was also unable to attack Moscow because a lack of the wherewithal to do so, caused by a combination of bad roads, *rasputitsa*, the poor railway lines – and, of course, Hitler's reworking of the military plan. HG Süd's advance was stopped after Kiev fell, thanks to the destruction of railway bridges across the Dnieper, partisan activity and chaos on the railways that cut the number of trains arriving to less than a quarter of those needed.

That the Germans were able to advance so far and sustain the offensives for so long in 1941 and 1942 speaks more for the professionalism, inventiveness and ability to live off the land of the German soldier than to the effectiveness of German logistics systems.

Opposite: Railways had been crucial during the First World War, allowing Germany to fight a two-front war. They would prove just as important in 1939–45. Various classes of *Kriegslokomotiven* (war locomotives) were produced in large numbers for the Deutsche Reichsbahn, many by forced labour, to meet Germany's transport needs. Technically, they were as simple as possible and avoided the use of scarce materials, copper in particular. The most-produced – 7,794 in total – was the Class 52. Many other, older locomotives were also used, including the Class 56 built as the Prussian G 8.2 in the 1920s. This photograph is of Locomotive No. 56 2318 pulling 168. Infanterie-Division towards Ukraine. Under XXXIV. Armeekorps the 168. Division saw action at the huge encirclement battle of Kiev.

Bw. Ly.
56 2318

Above: Two troop transport trains stop to let their passengers stretch their legs. German military trains were standardised, and H.G.W. Davie gives as an example the I Type composed of twenty-six flat cars, twenty-eight goods vans and a brake van which could carry 350 men, twenty vehicles and seventy horses. This sort of cargo load meant that an infantry division could be carried by seventy trains; a Panzer division in ninety. The locomotives are probably of Polish Railways (PKP) Class Ty23, a 2-10-0 that was built in large numbers. In 1939 after the conquest of Poland the Germans took over 438 of them and classified them as Class $58^{23-27}$. Further locos of the class were captured from the Russians during *Barbarossa*.

Opposite: The Soviets spirited away as many of the locomotives and as much of the rolling stock as they could – H.G.W. Davie quotes 22,200 locos saved and only 2,000 lost (and most of those were unserviceable). Almost as importantly, the Soviets destroyed all the infrastructure, particularly the depots where the locomotives were looked after. The Germans relaid the track to their own gauge and extended the lines along their main attack lines, but there was never sufficient capacity because the emphasis was on speed – keeping up with the advancing troops – rather than taking longer to create lines with a higher capacity. This train is composed of flat cars transporting assorted weaponry and motorcycles. Note the canvas covers for the 2cm Flak guns and the barrel plugs.

Above: *Ohne Mampf, kein Kampf* (without grub, no battle) or *Ohne Verpflegung, keine Bewegung* (without food no movement) – a good cook, hot food and plenty of it: essential for morale. Here a large army field kitchen readies its equipment preparatory to feeding the next batch of troops. Note the Sanka (ambulance) at right.

Opposite above: A supply train makes its way towards the front in 1944. For *Barbarossa*, the Wehrmacht was in control of the railways – there had been friction between the army and the Reichsverkehrsministerium (RVM – Ministry of Transport) after the French campaign. The Wehrmacht did not have the experience or the manpower to sort out the railways over such long distances and army logistics suffered. In 1942 control was handed back to the RVM but it took too long to make a difference when it counted. Davie writes, 'As late as June 1944 Heeresgruppe Mitte would have to choose between transporting munitions or reinforcements, as there was insufficient railway capacity to carry both simultaneously.' The Soviets, on the other hand, made excellent use of their rail resources and had far fewer logistical problems. Note the stake wagons; during the war the Germans concentrated the number of wagons they built into the *Kriegsbauart* (wartime class) to restrict the types being made.

Opposite below: A treat for a child? If so, it does not look too happy about it. This train is being prepared to head east from north Germany some time in 1944. The man leaning against the trailer wears the Sturmgeschütz/Sturmartillerie field-grey version of the black Panzer uniform with red piping.

While there was a culture of cycling in Germany, the Germans did not consider using bicycles for mass movement (unlike the Japanese). Nevertheless, they were extensively used throughout the war and well over a million of the Truppenfahrrad – the official German Army bicycle, with a strengthened carry rack above the rear wheel and a toolkit under the crossbar – were manufactured by more than thirty companies. This bicycle could also carry an ammunition box under the crossbar and was adapted to carry other equipment for military use: machine guns, mortars and anything else applicable. There was even a Red Cross version that could tow

a stretcher unit. The bicycles were used by recce groups and, later in the war, by the Volksgrenadiere and Volkssturm. From late 1943 they were used less for reconnaissance and more as a mobile reserve, heavily armed with Panzerfäuste. This is a medical detachment of 167. Infanterie-Division at Briansk in 1941. Note the two-bike stacking system, frequently seen, the tan medical pouches and the medical trade badge on the man in centre of the image.

A mixture of transport in the Soviet Union in 1941 as German soldiers shepherd PoWs. Note the *Zeltbahn* and helmet on handlebars, front light and all-black colour scheme. The road is typical of those found in the Soviet Union: compact good surfaces for much of the year, in the rainy season they became impassable quagmires.

Young but seasoned, German infantry move to the front in Ukraine in 1942. Note the Iron Cross 2nd Class ribbons on two of the NCOs at the head of the column and the silver Infantry Assault Badges (*Infanterie-Sturmabzeichen*) many are wearing. The central soldier has magazine pouches for his MP 42. There are various weapons, mainly Kar98k rifles and shoulder-carried MG 34s. Most of the infantry units marched to the front from railheads come rain, come shine. Their uniforms suffered and lice and other vermin were a constant problem.

Knackered! Weary, dusty infantrymen try to find some shade as they take a break from the heat during a route march. Contrary to mostly exaggerated claims and, subject to the conditions, task and weight carried, about 30km (20 miles) was the norm.

The most technically advanced army in Europe relied on four-legged horsepower to pull everything from artillery to the Gulaschkanone (mobile field kitchens) that fed them. In 1939 the Wehrmacht had 3,800,000 horses and as the war progressed, especially in the east, for every three horses two were needed to pull their feed. The Germans entered the Soviet Union with 625,000 horses. By the end of January 1941, 179,132 had died and nearly 30,000 were sick: almost a third in just over six months. This had a crippling effect on the horse-drawn army – especially as by then many of their wheeled vehicles were also out of service or frozen solid. Gregory Liedtke gives the example of Heeresgruppe Süd, which on 20 February 1942 had lost 23,526 of the motor vehicles with which it had started the campaign and of the 86,757 it still had, nearly 82 per cent were not operational.

Inset: In the first winter of 1941/42, Panzer divisions became 'panje divisions' because they became so dependent on their horses. The panje horse was a small, scruffy and hardy pony used to working in the harsh conditions of the Russian winter. They could not pull the weight of the draught horses, so consequently their sleds/carts were smaller but much more manoeuvrable. They needed less fodder and would survive with minimal shelter. The horse-drawn sleighs were life-savers for the Germans – winter transport for supplies and for getting the wounded evacuated from the front.

The horses in this photograph are too big and sturdy to be panjes – many of the larger European horses did not survive the winter.

Above: In 1939 Oberst (later Generalleutnant) Adolf von Schell – the Generalbevollmächtigten für das Kraftfahrwesen (General Plenipotentiary for Motor Vehicles) – produced a programme to reduce the number of vehicle types – trucks, cars and motorcycles – being produced by the numerous German manufacturers. On paper the number of lorry types was cut from 114 to 19, and passenger cars from 52 to 29 types. In reality, the Wehrmacht did not keep to this plan, especially when one takes into account captured vehicles or those from the conquered nations. This convoy of cargo truck and trailer combos crossing a ford is flagged *OKH Fernlast* – in other words, a vehicle providing long-distance transport at the behest of the OKH, usually carrying weapons, ammunition and equipment needed urgently at the front. A towing cable has been used on the vehicle in the foreground.

Opposite above: Well over half the German Army units at the start of the war were horse-drawn and the number grew. The army had a large cadre of veterinarians – over 5,000, about half of the total number of vets in Germany. It also had many soldiers from a rural background who were familiar with handling work horses in the fields, hunting or general duties such as draught horses or pulling brewery drays (*Brauereiwagen*). Horses require a lot of looking after and at least 6kg (13lb) of feed a day; large draught horses as much as 9kg (20lb) or eight hours' grazing if available. All told, that meant 4,500 tonnes of feed a day for the armies readied for *Barbarossa*. The truck is a captured Soviet Lend–Lease Studebaker US6 U-4.

Opposite below: The German cavalry numbers grew during the war, not just the army units but those of the Waffen-SS. There were also Hungarian cavalry and regiments of Cossacks that became the XV. SS-Kosaken-Kavallerie-Korps in 1945. The cavalry mounts were carefully chosen – training started at around four years and took on average two years to complete. A prewar cavalry man commented on the bond between man and horse as responsibility, comradeship and love. Prior to 1935 many hours were spent on basic rider training for the cavalry, thus setting the standard for mounted troops. At the outbreak of war they were tasked as reconnaissance battalions. Looking after the horses was, of course, essential. Grooming got rid of fleas and ticks, and helped identify any health issues. As a cavalryman noted, the infantry when on the march will get a break from time to time and have their routines; for the cavalryman this means watering his mount and checking it over as its needs come first before he can rest.

Mercedes-Benz Type 3000S light cargo truck with trailer. Note the *WH* – Wehrmacht – identification. *Barbarossa* stuttered in September and October 1941, a victim of its own success. Having advanced so far so quickly, there had been few opportunities to overhaul or repair vehicles. As the supply lines got further away from the railheads, so the attrition on motor vehicles – as well as the *rasputitsa* – forced the Panzer divisions to slow as horses had to take over the transport of supplies to the front.

The Krupp Protze (*Protze* means ammunition limber) had the official designation L2H143 (L = *Lastwagen* – lorry, 2 = load capacity in tonnes, H = light frame, 1 = first change from the basic 43 (so 243 would be the second version), 43 = 4-cylinder, 3 axles). Seven thousand Protzes were built between 1934 and 1941 and many were used as artillery tractors. When used in combination with the 3.7cm Panzerabwehrkanone (PaK) 36 (nicknamed the 'door-knocker' because of its inability to destroy Russian tanks at range), the Protze was designated Kfz 69. (The infantry transport version was Kfz 70.)

1,500 Dodge VH-48 3-ton trucks were delivered to the French Army in April/May 1940. They had hardly arrived before they became part of the German inventory – as was so much French equipment. Part of the rationale for German conquest was the booty they needed to prop up their economy. This VH-48 is pictured near Stalingrad in 1942. Note the missing numberplate and the markings on the fenders that show it is from a signals unit.

The Dunkirk debacle saw the British abandon 64,000 trucks and vehicles in France; others were captured in Greece and North Africa. Many of them would see service with the German Army throughout the war. These examples show: (Above) a British Morris Commercial PU 8cwt, 4 x 4 lorry in use by II./Artillerie-Regiment 63 (note the unit identification on the front mudguard). Originally equipped with 15cm sFH 18s (schwere Feldhaubitze – heavy howitzer), in 1943, the unit re-equipped with the Hummel SP gun. (Below) A captured Bedford OYD 3-ton general service vehicle being cleaned by a Luftwaffe ground unit in Romania in 1941.

Halftracks were important prime movers for artillery and to carry infantry (later Panzergrenadiers) in Panzer divisions. Although much artillery was horse-drawn, it was a lot easier to pull the heavies with vehicles. However, as early designs such as the 15cm sFH 18 heavy field howitzer were designed to be towed by horse, they had unsprung axles and hard rubber tyres. To allow them to be towed, a two-wheel bogie was designed. This worked well although the lack of springs meant that the speed had to be kept low. The heaviest German halftrack was the 18-ton SdKfz 9 Famo (Fahrzeug und Motorenbau GmbH) prime mover, seen here pulling an sFH 18 with its crew of seven. Some of the heaviest guns had to be transported in separate pieces (barrel and mount). Note the untouched landscape of the early days of *Barbarossa*.

20
K
10

Opposite above: This SdKfz 9 is pulling a Tiefladeanhänger für Panzerkampfwagen 10t – the Sonder-Anhänger (SdAh, special trailer) 115 – a low-loading trailer for vehicles up to 10 tonnes in weight. This could cope with most light armoured vehicles, having been designed to be able to take the PzKpfw II. Heavier trailers included the SdAh 116 22-ton tank transporter trailer with a driver-operated independent-powered steerable unit at the rear, the SdAh 118 45-ton and SdAh 121 68-ton – the latter being necessary for the Tiger II although the towing speed of about 10km/h (6mph) meant it was not very useful for tactical movements. The SdKfz 9 had a pulling weight of 28 tonnes, enough for most PzKpfw IVs although two, three or four prime movers were needed in heavy conditions.

Opposite below: The SdKfz 10 was the smallest of the prime movers, the most numerous – some 14,000 built – and possibly the most versatile. Its principal role was towing the smaller guns: for example, the 7.5cm PaK 40 anti-tank gun or 28/32cm Nebelwerfer 14 rocket launcher. This one carries a range of tactical markings showing: K for Panzergruppe 1 (originally Panzergruppe *von Kleist*), underneath that the symbol for 3. Armee-Korps; at right top the yellow 14. Panzer-Division marking (the same as 4. Infanterie-Division because the division was formed from that and Panzer-Regiment 36 from 4. Panzer-Division) and below that, in white, those for 10./Schützen-Regiment 103. Behind the halftrack there are assorted motorcycles with sidecars and a 4 x 4 Horch medium car. Panzergruppe 1 saw action in Heeresgruppe Süd for most of the latter half of 1941.

Below: Motorbike despatch riders (*Kradmelder*) of 22. Panzer-Division on the Don front in 1942. In the early days of Blitzkrieg – especially in western Europe where the roads were good – the German Army employed motorcycles for numerous jobs from despatch riding to reconnaissance. Attaching a machine gun to the sidecar gave considerable firepower and their mobility proved effective in the early months of *Barbarossa* as they could carry a sizeable load at 18km/litre (45 miles per gallon) until the *rasputitsa* bogged them. 22. Panzer-Division was part of the advance and capture of Rostov-on-Don, gateway to the Caucasus.

A 297. Infanterie-Division carpool outside Stalingrad. In the foreground, with its front seats removed for cleaning, is an Audi Front 225 – the early Audi logo is visible on the radiator. The sign reads *Markt und Ausstellungsplatz der Stadtgemeinde Bruck an der Leitha* – Market and Exhibition Hall of the Town of Bruck an der

Leitha, a town in Austria. The river Leitha flows into the Danube – a long way from Stalingrad. But 297. Infanterie-Division was set up at Bruck, so some wit with time on his hands has marked their spot accordingly! The division was destroyed at Stalingrad, rebuilt later in 1943 at Bordeaux and fought for the rest of the war in the Balkans.

Inset: Part of the drive to reduce the number of types of vehicle available to the Wehrmacht to increase standardisation and make spare parts more easily used, a 1934 plan to create the Einheits-Pkw – a standard passenger vehicle – proposed three classes of all-wheel-drive vehicles: *leichte* (light), *mittlerer* (medium) and *schwere* (heavy). The only successful type was the *mittlerer*, designated Kfz 12, which included the Horch 901, one of which is seen here in hastily whitewashed camouflage near Kharkov in 1942. Nearly 15,000 of these were built, from 1940 on with an internal spare wheel and wider body. These versatile vehicles were used to tow light guns, carry personnel and, most importantly, as a commander's vehicle.

The German equivalent of the jeep – although with only around 50,000 manufactured as against over 600,000, the comparison is stretched – the Type 82 Kübelwagen (tub or bucket car) was a 4 x 2 with steel doors based on the VW Beetle. A light cross-country car, it had the advantage that, when empty, it could be manhandled by four men if stuck in the mud. Some 15,000 of the amphibious version – the Schwimmwagen – were also built. Note the *dunkelgelb/olivgrün* camouflage on the vehicle by the building. The photograph was taken in March 1945 during *Unternehmen Frühlingserwachen* around Lake Balaton (which the Germans called the Plattensee) in Hungary.

Enemy action is always a big problem for soft-skinned transport vehicles – particularly at the spearhead of the advance or with enemy air assets roving behind the front line. It is an especial problem for armoured vehicles fighting in a built-up area, where they can easily be ambushed unless there is massive infantry

support. Here a convoy passes two knocked-out halftracks from 297. Infanterie-Division that have been moved out of the path.

Railways are always a good target for aviation and artillery but much of the damage done to Soviet railway infrastructure – in particular, bridges, signal boxes, watering points, locomotive depots and works – was carried out by partisans or by the Red Army itself as it retreated. This is Kharkov in 1942, a fortress city with a predominantly Ukrainian population. In October 1942 after fierce fighting, the Russians abandoned it, destroying much of the infrastructure as they retreated.

The T-34, designed by Mikhail Koshkin, was first produced at the Kharkov Comintern Locomotive Plant before the works were forced to relocate to the Ural mountains after the German invasion.

Inset: Train crashes happen in war or peace but head-on collisions are pretty rare. This one was between two supply trains and involved Kraftfahrersatzabteilung 45 (motor vehicle replacement detachment).

Above: Terrain causes logistics problems. This *dunkelgelb/olivgrün* camouflaged Ford v8/51 tanker is carefully negotiating a river crossing. The Axis forces used a number of different tankers, one of the best known – more associated with the Luftwaffe – was the Opel Flugbetriebsstoff Kessel-Kraftwagen (Tankwagen) Kfz 385, which could pull a specially developed trailer (Anh B2/1).

Opposite above: Hard at work, mechanics of a signals detachment of 225. Infanterie-Division (the divisional insignia is just visible on the vehicle on the right) work to keep their vehicles on the road. Keeping passenger cars – particularly requisitioned (civilian) vehicles – serviceable was a major drain on maintenance crews. Note the winter boots and tyre pressure (1 Atü = 15 psi). The 225. Division fought around Leningrad in 1942 and ended the war in the Courland pocket.

Opposite below: Fuel was a scarce commodity at times on the Eastern Front, particularly if you had outrun your supply lines. In the field, fuelling up was a long and laborious process, usually via a hand pump that could provide 60 litres (13 gallons) a minute for fuel (Kraftstoffhandpumpe – KHP), and 40 litres (9 gallons) a minute for lubricating oil (Schmierstoffhandpumpe). The Luftwaffe units – because they were on airfields and usually static – used the heavier KHP 4; the army the lighter KHP 2. There was an oil-trailer (Öltankwagen mit Handbetrieb) that held 300 litres (66 gallons) for Luftwaffe use. The army more commonly used 200-litre (44-gallon) fuel drums with distinctive 'rolling' rings or the iconic 20-litre (4-gallon) 'jerrycan'. Copied by every side, the style is still used today. Weighing in at 20kg (45lb) when full, it was the primary method of fuelling while on the move. The 200-litre fuel drums, stamped Wehrmacht, Luftwaffe or Kriegsmarine, would be either on trailers of one or two axles or (as here) on the back of a truck, often an Opel Blitz. The drums would have been offloaded at a rail depot, loaded by hand up a double-plank ramp and then be allocated at a fuel depot, where the fuel was hand-pumped into jerrycans.

Men of 212. Infanterie-Division manhandle a narrow-gauge wagon along a corduroy trackbed. A corduroy road is constructed from logs laid side by side transversely, covered with whatever is available or, in this case, nothing as the bolted rail tracks bind them. No army wants to fight in, or even cross, marshland and as Operation *Barbarossa* moved forward the Wehrmacht was no different. The Pripet Marshes (Pripjet-Sumpfe in German) are the largest area of wetland in Europe. Along the Ukraine–Belarus border, covering an area of 269,400km$^2$ (104,000 sq miles), it was a barrier skirted on the advance. In retreat, a number of German divisions had to cut their way through using corduroy roads. Note the mosquito nets some personnel are wearing. 212. Division was moved to the Soviet Union in October 1941 and took part in the siege of Leningrad, fighting on the shores of Lake Ladoga. Decimated in Lithuania, the unit was disbanded in September 1944, its personnel going on to form 212. Volksgrenadier-Division. Friedrich Sander said this on the way north: '[We] scare out the mosquitoes by smoking some papyrossis or a cigar. After the rainfall, however, the masses of mosquitoes swarmed about. The beasts know how to find even the smallest patch of uncovered skin. "Ssssss", they land and then one can hear the distinctive "smack" of a hand often followed by some juicy curse. Now, however, we have reached an area where not only the mosquitoes bite. There are cleg-flies, gadflies from the corpses and fat horseflies and all those are determined to stab you. It's not uncommon to see men with swollen hands, cheeks and eyes. The beasts are everywhere! I hope there are none in Leningrad.' The *papyrossis* he mentions are Russian cigarette invented in the nineteenth century, where a small paper tube holds tobacco, atop a cardboard tube that can be pinched to make a cigarette holder.

The season of bad roads known in Russian as *rasputitsa* is a combination of rapid thawing with the rains of spring or the deluges of autumn that makes unpaved roads and tracks all but impassable. It is particularly bad in Ukraine, and in 1941 brought the Germans crashing to a halt – although supply and maintenance problems also contributed. The sort of difficulties experienced are well shown in the photograph of a Zündapp KS750 combo motorcycle being manhandled through heavy mud. Both the Zündapp and BMW R75 proved the equal of most things the Russian weather could fling at them, but ultimately they were too expensive to produce as compared to the Kübelwagen, and it took over.

The other obvious weather problem in the Soviet Union was snow. Chained wheels were needed for pushing and clearing snow, even for a lightweight truck to pull a snowplough – irony in action. Considered a defensive advantage for centuries 'General Winter' earned its reputation by hindering the German Army as it advanced into Russia.

# 2 Behind the Front Lines

THERE WAS ALWAYS A plan for the east, but it did not involve winning over the population. And yet there was a real opportunity in some areas where the Kremlin's rule had brought death and poverty. Ukraine, for example, had endured the Holodomor in 1932–33, the famine that, if it was not manmade, was certainly not helped by Stalin's policies. The Baltic states the Soviets had walked into in 1940 were also ripe for rebellion. In Russia itself, while most had taken up the communist cause, there were many – particularly the kulaks and other groups persecuted by Stalin – who were ready to be won over by 'liberators'.

The Nazis were anything but liberators. They had a plan – *Generalplan Ost* – and it involved extermination: particularly of the Jews, Poles and Slavs. Subsequently, as German settlers took over the lands that had been ethnically cleansed, those Slavs who survived would be forced to work as slaves for the master race. While the Nazis did their level best to destroy all references to *Generalplan Ost* towards the end of the war as the Allies' noose on their empire tightened, sufficient information remained for it to be pieced together.

To effect this plan, the first step was to control what the Germans had won and begin the extermination. The killings were orchestrated by the Einsatzgruppen, the death squads that followed each army and were assisted by them. As far as the countless PoWs streaming back from the front or the civilian population were concerned, this meant mass starvation and extermination. Those who were left – and were too racially impure to be 'Germanised' – were destined to be forcibly sent to the east. The raw materials and anything useful to the Reich were to be sent west. The rest was to be destroyed and the land settled by German farmers.

The administration that followed the military was divided into four Reichskommissariate – similar to those set up in Norway, the Netherlands and Belgium/northern France – Ostland (the Baltic states and Belarus), Ukraine, Kaukasien (southern Russia and the Caucasus) and Moskowien (the rest of European Russia less those bits that went to Finland). Only Ostland and Ukraine were set up completely and were able to advance fully the extermination of the Jews and movement of slave labour to the Reich.

Between the invasion and 1945, the Germans had enough time to put much of *Generalplan Ost* into effect: the genocide, the use of slave labour, the looting of the countries they conquered. Behind them, as they retreated, they left scorched earth and a hasty cover-up of as many of their iniquities as they could.

As this photograph taken by a 22. Panzer-Division tank driver implies, the Germans could have won hearts and minds when they entered Ukraine. Many treated them as liberators. The Germans, however, had no intention of treating any of the Soviet peoples with an iota of kindness. As the army moved through, so the Einsatzgruppen moved in to exterminate the Jews. Following on were the agencies that exploited the resources of the conquered lands. By instituting a regime of terror, the Germans played into Soviet hands, and the communists were able to keep the population onside.

Railheads were the key to supplying the field forces. If it were possible, railheads down to division were set up, but with the railheads being an average of 160km (100 miles) from the front lines, most were at Armee or Korps level. At the railheads, supplies were loaded up for onward delivery. This photograph shows munitions awaiting onward distribution. The bombs seen here are Splitterbomben (fragmentation bombs with a thicker casing), SD 250kg or 500kg from the SD 70 series in sledge frames. They have dark grey casing for normal climates (different climates had different colours). There are assorted calibre crates behind and small trucks being loaded at the rear.

The quieter areas behind the front were the locations for supply dumps. First came the army dumps – *Lager* – and, if the front line were too far away, corps *Lager* were introduced. The next level down were the divisional distribution centres, the Ausgabestelle, for rations, fuel and ammunition – here an ammunition distribution point for 19. Panzer-Division (identified by the rune below the sign). Each of the signs identifies a unit: for example, in the centre is the symbol for Brückenkolonne B (or Brüko, motorised bridging column (mot)). Armies and divisions also maintained collecting points (Sammelstellen), where new or repaired equipment was handed over and damaged or captured equipment was collected. Note the female local in the middle distance. She may be curious, foraging or even spying and reporting back to partisan or resistance groups.

A strategy meeting being held by 22. Panzer-Division's Aufklärungs-Abteilung (recce battalion; note the *goldgelb Waffenfarbe*) in Rostov-on-Don in July 1942, shortly after the city had been taken. 22. Panzer-Division had not performed well since its arrival in the east and was about to undergo a reorganisation with elements being used to create Kampfgruppe *Michalik*, which later became the basis for 27. Panzer-Division.

The events that followed the first Battle of Kharkov in mid-October 1941 typify the German occupation of the Soviet Union. The Germans took control of the city on 24 October and immediately initiated a campaign of murder against communists. On 14 November, a number of time-bombs left by the Red Army detonated, killing many of 68. Infanterie-Division's staff and its commander, Generalleutnant Georg Braun. Retribution was swift and terrible. About 200 innocent civilians, mainly Jews, were hung from balconies on the larger buildings by the Wehrmacht troops. Another thousand or so were held in the International Hotel as hostages. The hotel, seen in November 1942 with a Luftwaffe guard, had been opened in 1936. It was a grand affair: 495 rooms, a banquet hall and restaurants, and in 1937 it won the Grand Prix for interior design at the World Exhibition of Arts and Technology in Paris. When Einsatzgruppe C arrived there, they shot the remaining hostages. Just under two years later, the Germans were forced out of the city. The reign of terror had included public executions, the murder of 10,000 Jews and starvation of the population.

The German units planned to counter disaffection in rear areas with the security divisions – Sicherungs-Divisionen. But initially only nine were raised (in the end there were fifteen, of which one served in France). They had an impossible job. There were too few men and most were unsuited to the demands of anti-partisan duties: unfit, too old (in January 1943, the average age of new officers transferred to 203. Sicherungs-Division was nearly 48) and with poor weaponry. Added to this, the vast areas of often inhospitable terrain – lakes, mosquitoes, rivers and swamps – were perfect for partisan activities. The Sicherungs-Divisionen, usually split up into battalions, answered with violence. Mass killing became the norm. The photograph shows men of Sicherungs-Bataillon 738 under command of Heeresgruppe Mitte with a Hiwi on the railway line between Bryansk and Konotop in Ukraine.

Over 3.5 million Soviet soldiers were taken prisoner in 1941. They were collected into huge camps (above) – this one overlooked by an SdKfz 10/5 with 20mm Flak 38. Developed in the 1930s, the halftrack had a flatbed with side and rear panels that dropped to increase platform size, and underneath these were spare 20-round box magazines (seen here). As the war progressed, it became less effective as an anti-aircraft (AA) gun but remained an effective infantry support weapon.

The accepted number of Soviet PoWs taken into German captivity during the war is 5.7–6 million. On top of this, some 500,000 were killed after surrendering. Two-thirds of those who became PoWs died in captivity, most of the deaths in 1941 were as a result of maltreatment or murder by Wehrmacht forces. Soviet PoWs were trapped in a no-win situation. As far as Stalin was concerned, there were no PoWs, just traitors. On the other hand, a mixture of neglect, disease, their jailers' murderous intent and the sheer numbers meant that life expectancy for a Soviet PoW in German hands was very poor: only a third of Soviets who became PoWs survived the war. The least likely to stay alive were Jews (as here below, photographed in 1942), commissars and – to a lesser extent – officers (here a lieutenant opposite).

The Germans were able to recruit Hiwi auxiliaries, which was an attractive alternative to remaining as a PoW. Hiwis proliferated as the war went on, as Nazi dogma, which was opposed to making use of these *Untermenschen* as soldiers, was pragmatically toned down when more hands were needed. Hiwis served in many roles including as executioners and facilitators of the Final Solution – or, as here (opposite below), carrying supplies for 3. Panzer-Division in 1942.

Most of the time Hiwis volunteered rather than face death and not for ideological reasons. This did not help them when the war ended. The Soviet authorities treated them as might be expected and the gulags' ranks swelled until Krushchev's amnesty of 1954. Note the home-made armbands: (opposite above) *Im Dienst der Deutschen Wehrmacht* (In service of the German armed forces) and (above) *Wehrmacht Gehilfe* (German armed forces assistant). The happy Hiwi wears a Soviet greatcoat, a Russian tanker's protective headwear and a variation of a volunteer armband.

While the Hiwis were nominally volunteers and therefore freely gave assistance to the Wehrmacht, there were also many, many who did not volunteer. The Germans rounded up thousands to be used as forced labour, as distinct from slave labourers – the former received something for their efforts. The slave labourers, men and women alike, were those who until 1942 had simply been murdered or exterminated in camps. There came a time, however, when manpower shortages forced the Nazis to make use of their captives by working them to death rather than killing them outright. The images here are of forced labourers heading to work in a Czechoslovak factory (above), and Soviet PoWs building a bunker for a Panzer unit during the winter of 1941/42 – sawn timber can be seen in the background – although the Geneva Convention of 1929 stated that work by PoWs should not be war-related (oposite).

European Russia did not have a highway system comparable to the west's. The best roads were either cobbled (as here) or asphalted, but only in or leading to major areas of commerce and industry. Most of the roads had no surface other than what was there. In summer there were clouds of dust, in winter, snow and ice, then after a thaw impassable mud.

The tractor in the right-hand middle distance is the widely used military version of the Soviet agricultural workhorse Stalinets-65 SG-65, used for hauling artillery and well suited for local conditions (mud and snow). Most Russian soldiers were familiar with this type of machinery. Note the lack of spare wheel on the rear of the motorcycle combination.

Above: Traffic control is a crucial factor in war, for example to ensure that all elements of an attack reach their jumping-off positions on time, or to allow a continuous supply of ammunition, food and fuel to troops in combat. Concentrations of troops in transit are vulnerable to air attack and, as they get closer to the front, artillery – particularly if they are snarled up in a traffic jam. Behind the front lines, partisans attacked many a straggler from a supply column. German Army traffic control was usually handled by the Feldgendarmerie, whose main tasks were to post signs and mark routes; control traffic at key points; reroute traffic in emergencies or when the tactical situation changed; and supervise all movements to the rear along designated routes such as barrier and straggler lines. Here, a soldier from Kraftfahr-Abteilung 562 uses a Feldgendarmerie traffic-control paddle to direct traffic. Originally set up in 1939 as Nachschub-Kolonnen-Abteilung 562 and deployed in the west, from 1941 it became part of 17. Armee on the Eastern Front. It was renamed Kraftfahr-Abteilung 562 in January 1943 and destroyed in the Crimea.

As well as enemy action, mud was a continual problem. The *raputitsa* made the poor Soviet road system impassable. The mud in this photograph is not too bad, although the mud-spattered soldier at right who has had to help unbog a vehicle may have thought otherwise. The horse and cart, meanwhile, have no problems negotiating the mud or the traffic.

Opposite above: The paramilitary Reichsarbeitsdienst saw young men serve for six months of drill, military-themed training and general toughening up before starting their time in the military proper. During the war they were increasingly employed in work related to the armed forces as Wehrmachtsgefolge (auxiliaries). Their uniform had a brown collar as seen and the Model 1943 field cap with their distinctive insignia – an upturned spade with two corn-heads underneath – giving rise to the motto *Mit Spaten und Ähre* (with spades and ears of corn). These RAD men are queuing for soup or a stew being ladled from a version of the double-skinned aluminium flask (*Essentrager*).

Opposite below: A PzKpfw III Ausf J of 5. SS-Panzer-Division *Wiking* (the divisional sign is on the right front mudflap: a swastika variant of the ancient sun cross runic symbol). With its ranks including many northern European volunteers, the division was ordered east in May 1941, to join Heeresgruppe Süd's advance into Ukraine. There it gained a reputation for brutality.

There are some anxious looks forward and back; the spades and loose soil suggest that some crater-filling might have taken place.

Poltawa
179
Ost u. West

Traffic control is helped by clear signage – and these look anything but! The red cross on white background obviously indicates medical facilities. The others are a mixture of military directions. The lowest at left shows *Panzerstraße Ost und West* – towards which the PzKpfw III in the photograph is heading. The top sign is for Poltava, a city west of Kharkhiv.

The Feldgendarmerie's distinctive gorget hung around the neck on a chain – giving them the nickname of the 'chained dogs'. This motorcycle MP has his traffic-control paddle and awaits the unit he is working for. Controlling traffic at key points like this was a major part of his job. In the foreground a work party from 19. Panzer-Division works on graves of their fallen comrades. The birchwood surrounds and the helmets on the crosses can be seen. The pennant and 1b lettering indicate the location of the divisional supply group. Run by the second staff officer (1b), the group was responsible for the supply of the division.

The 7.5cm Sturmgeschütz (StuG) 40 Ausf G was as much a tank-killer as an assault gun. This one, however, has a broken front drive-wheel and the forward movement from the other side has thrown the track. This one-sided forward momentum has also forced the road wheels to clog up. The photo suggests that this happened in a quiet sector with no great urgency to recover, thus the muzzle cover and canvas top-cover. The Germans worked hard to ensure that damaged vehicles were repaired and reintroduced to the front line; only complete write-offs were scrapped. If the crew could not resolve the problem, the tank company's maintenance detachment would try. Failing that, the vehicle would be recovered to a suitable workshop for heavier work.

A tank regiment's maintenance company has set up shop. In the foreground, a PzKpfw III Ausf J with a 5cm KwK L/42 gun. Note 9. Panzer-Division tactical marking above and to the right of the driver's vision slit. There is another PzKpfw III, turretless, to the right. The gantry behind would be capable of lifting the turret or engine as necessary. Everyone came to respect the mechanics. Friedrich Sander wrote: 'I have made sure that everything ... went straight to Panzer mechanic Hoppmann of the 5th Company who today, a Sunday

has been slaving away like mad. That boy and his mates are constantly at work, without having the time to enjoy any of the few comforts we soldiers are able to get hold of out here. When we called him into our cottage, Hoppmann was wondering what else he was supposed to do for us, but then he made big eyes when the nice, fat potatoes were offered to him.'

Above: The same area from a different angle, with two PzKpfw IIs (left and right) and, behind the tree, No. 634, a PzKpfw IV. Tank crews spent a lot of time trying to ensure that their machines kept running, but in action it was an uphill struggle. A thrown track was bread and butter for them, just an occupational hazard. Damage by enemy action was another thing altogether, as were major automotive issues.

Tank recovery vehicles were scarce. Once the vehicle – and crew – reached the tank maintenance company, the vehicle would be repaired and sent back into action. The crew would wait for their vehicle or be posted – together or individually – to other vehicles.

Opposite above: The Sicherungs-Divisionen (initially three for each of three Heeresgruppen) were to systematically purge dispersed enemy elements; arrest civilians suspected of collaborating with the enemy; and prevent or crush terrorist groups. Soldiers in plain clothes, often simply identified as being men with short haircuts, were to be shot; Jews were to be shot; civilians were to be shot. In fact, pretty much anyone was to be shot. One commander reported in March 1942 that nearly 64,000 'partisans' had been shot. The likelihood is that few if any were actually partisans. It was anti-partisan warfare without any partisans being involved. In July 1942, the SS took over and partisans became 'bandits' and anti-partisan warfare became *Bandenbekämpfung*. A Bandit Warfare Badge (*Bandenkampfabzeichen*) was awarded from 29 January 1944. The effect of this repression? Huge numbers of villages burnt, civilians murdered – and a rise in the number of partisans, from small numbers in 1941 to over half a million in 1943.

Hangings were for the benefit of the local population – an official notification giving the reason for the punishment would be nailed to a post, bottom right-hand corner, or hung around the neck. The hangings shown are by strangulation, a cruel way to kill, instead of a short drop to break the neck and death.

Opposite below: R&R – rest and relaxation – is an important factor in maintaining morale, particularly at Christmas. *Weihnachten* presented the Nazis with an interesting dilemma. Senior Nazis – such as Himmler – were very anti-church. Certainly, for political reasons, the Nazis were hostile to much of the Catholic Church. One aspect of Nazi ideology was to 'Nazify' Christmas because Jesus was a Jew. With Germany being a devoutly Christian nation, this was only partially successful and the Nazis were forced to turn a blind eye to certain traditions, the Christmas tree in particular, as long as it did not have a star of David on top! As the candles are lit by an infantry Hauptmann (captain), the presents from home are ready to open – many will be chocolates and tobacco.

The cauldron at Stalingrad was a line of defence about 50km (30 miles) wide and 30km (20 miles) deep. Within it were seven airfields receiving supplies – food and ammunition being the priority – for the 250,000-strong 6. Amee. The Luftwaffe had been tasked to supply a minimum of 500 tonnes per day. There was no way it was possible, even if they used every aircraft they had. At least half the aircraft were not fully operational at any one time; add to that the weather and the Red Air Force, and the airbridge was doomed to failure.

There was one limited success – the evacuation of the wounded and others. About 9,000 to 10,000 were evacuated by air. They were the priority as they had done their duty and were also useless mouths. Included in this number were specialists with highly technical skills. The photo shows horse-drawn covered ambulance sleds (Krankenschlitten), basically a shed on a sledge, waiting to move on.

The horse-drawn army: a pair of draught horses for each medical HF.7 Stahlfeldwagen (steel field wagons). These weighed about a ton each, with loading space of 2.5m$^3$ (88 cu ft) allowing a payload of around 1.5 tonnes – quite a weight with only two horses pulling, which is why they gained a bad reputation, especially in poor going. They could, however, be towed by motor vehicles or pulled by four horses. Note the padlocked sideboxes.

The field dressing station (Hauptverbandplatz) was the second port of call after the battalion aid post (Verwundetennest), where the trained medical NCO (Sanitätsunteroffizier) would assess the condition of the casualty, patch him up or pass him to the next level. This dressing station is well camouflaged: while the red

cross had an International meaning, it was not always observed in the east. The two ambulances look like horse-drawn types, narrow wheels and a step-up at the back. They both carry the tactical symbols for infantry along with white, black-out markings.

'Sankas' – shortened from *Sanitätskraftwagen*, ambulances – discharging their wounded. The Geneva Convention of 1929 exempted properly designed and marked vehicles from being fired upon. They had to be clearly marked like those in the photo. The Wehrmacht used a variety of vehicles in the role of ambulances (many identified as Kfz 31), the most well-known probably being the Opel Blitz. The trucks in this photograph are a Steyr 640 6 x 4 and two Ford G917t 4 x 2s. By 1939 each Armee had two medical companies (reduced to one as the war progressed), each of 200 personnel or so, and thirty to thirty-five ambulances.

Orderlies prepare to load a stretcher onto an ambulance. The German Red Cross was under the control of the Ministry of the Interior's Social Welfare Organisation, which was in reality a Nazi entity – in other words, it

had lost its independence and neutrality. As the nurse's Red Cross armband is not visible (it was nearly always worn on the left arm) and she is not wearing the traditional blue-striped blouse, she might be an auxiliary.

Hitler was not a frequent visitor to the front lines and most of the images of him in conquered territory – for example in Paris – were on visits well after the fighting was over. In the east, the two main headquarters (Führerhauptquartiere, FHQu) he used were the Wolfsschanze (Wolf's Lair), near Rastenburg in east Prussia and for periods in 1942 and 1943, Werwolf (Werewolf), north-east of Vinnytsia in Ukraine. He also visited Heeresgruppe Süd HQ at Mariupol in Ukraine in December 1941, when this photograph was taken. In the background is Felix Steiner, commander of SS-Division *Wiking*.

Opposite: Training is a continuous process for any army, and for one sustaining large casualties it was essential to bed in replacements and for officer candidate training, etc. New equipment required instruction, as did new tactics against enemy innovations. To begin with, this training took place in centres in Germany. After the initial territorial gains in 1939–41, centres were set up in conquered territories as well. On-the-spot training would take place within units' replacement battalions or even in situ. In this photo taken in early 1943 in Ukraine, a PzKpfw III Ausf L is used in anti-tank training. Note the camouflage colours of *dunkelgelb*, with secondary colours of *rotbraun* and *olivgrün*.

## The Luftwaffe

A brilliant opening assault on the VVS – the Red Air Force – saw the Luftwaffe destroy 2,000 Soviet aircraft. At a stroke, they achieved what their advancing Panzergruppen needed: battlefield air superiority. They did not have it all their own way, but they were able to assist materially the armoured thrusts and the great encirclement battles that followed.

That being said, as with the land forces, the Germans underestimated the Soviets. The VVS had also suffered from purges and reorganisations that contributed to it being unready for war. German intelligence identified this and, with all the arrogance shown by people who believed in their own racial superiority, failed to recognise the skills, improvisational abilities and bravery of the Red Air Force. The resilience the Soviets showed, the speed with which they recovered from the opening setbacks and their acceptance of huge losses to stop the invaders kept the Germans from being able to kill them off.

The underestimation of Soviet abilities is no better shown than by the assumption that Soviet industry would be unable to produce more than 600 aircraft a month when the real figure was around six times as many. The quality of Soviet aircraft was also underplayed, although by the end of the war the Luftwaffe knew better than to tangle with Yak-3 and Yak-9 fighters unless at a tactical advantage.

Also a problem was the German concentration on tactical requirements rather than strategic. With few long-range reconnaissance aircraft and bombers, and an increasing lack of transport aircraft, Luftwaffe aces might be able to accumulate large kill figures but they were unable to resupply the 6. Armee in Stalingrad as had been promised, or to come anywhere close to being able to bomb Soviet industrial sites. And, in the face of the Red Air Force, they could do little to stop the advances of the Red Army in 1944 and 1945.

Nowhere is that better shown than around Lake Balaton in 1945 when the Red Air Force contributed significantly to the blunting of German attempts to relieve Budapest. The Il-2 Sturmoviks of Soviet 17th Air Army owed their success to the bravery of their crew, the durability of their aircraft and the effectiveness of their PTAB (anti-tank) and FAB (general-purpose) bombs – a story that was repeated across the Eastern Front in the final months of the war.

Opposite above: The Eastern Front was vast, stretching from the Arctic Circle to the Caucasus. This is the Eismeergeschwader (Arctic Sea Fighter Wing) at Petsamo airfield in Finland. The aircraft are Bf 109Es of Jagdgeschwader 5, a unit that claimed some 3,200 kills during the war for the loss of 435 killed in action or taken prisoner.

Opposite below: *Schwarze 7*, a Bf 109G-6 of 2./NAGr. 12 – the 2. Staffel of Nahaufklärungsgruppe (Close Air Reconnaissance Group) 12 – in spring 1944. The unit was formed at the beginning of April 1943 in Herzogenaurach, Bavaria from 2.(H)/AufklGr 10 *Tannenberg*, which flew Focke-Wulf Fw 189 Uhu reconnaissance aircraft. In December 1943, the Staffel moved to Mostar in Bosnia, where it would remain until August 1944. The Germans had problems with photographic intelligence in the east. They attributed it to the Soviets' skill at camouflage, good road discipline and troop movements at night. A postwar analysis of German operational intelligence suggested: 'Perhaps a more accurate explanation was the lack of planes and equipment in the German Army, their poor technique, and the inadequacy of their personnel, both in quantity and training.' Finally, and importantly, German photo-interpretation was never really well developed or organised. This photo is from a sequence showing a Luftwaffe unit working on runway repairs.

7

Above: Over 5,500 Heinkel He 111s were built between 1939 and 1945 and they proved initially to be excellent jacks of all trades. Not as fast as the Ju 88, the He 111 also proved to be less adaptable. During the siege of Stalingrad they were pulled off bombing duties to help with the airlift and by the end of the war the aircraft was showing its age and was being used mainly for transport roles. Three Kampfgeschwader of He 111s were employed conventionally at the start of *Barbarossa*. Thereafter it acted as tank-buster, transport aircraft and long-range bomber as required. Friedrich Sander noted in his diary on 22 July 1941: 'Twenty-five German bombers are returning home from a mission. ... They are racing back to their airfield and our best wishes accompany them. Since the start of the campaign in the East our Landsers have learned to respect the Luftwaffe. All along the Rollbahn we have seen what even a single bomber can do to a marching column. One fighter after another is now returning. The yellow band around their fuselages and the yellow wingtips are glowing in the sunlight. Everyone is delighted to see them.' The yellow band is visible on this He 111H.

Opposite above: Messerschmitt Bf 109F-4 of the 5/2. Jagdstaffel (Fighter Squadron) of the Magyar Királyi Honvéd Légier (Royal Hungarian Air Force). Hitler was not enamoured with the Hungarians and in 1942 felt their air force's accomplishments paltry. Stephen Renner quotes him as saying, 'If I am going to give some aircraft, then rather to the Croats, who have proved they have an offensive spirit. To date we have only experienced fiascos with the Hungarians.' However, some second-hand aircraft were provided in 1942 and later in 1943 a joint aircraft production programme agreed in 1941 provided the Hungarians with Bf 109s and Me 210s. 5/2. Jagdstaffel transitioned onto the Bf 109 in early 1942, when this photograph was taken (note the lack of winter camouflage on the aircraft). The squadron would quickly start flying operationally, conducting ground-attack sorties with 250kg bombs in Ukraine. Renner reports they had twenty aerial victories during the Battle of Kursk, and a total of 132 Soviet aircraft destroyed by the end of 1943.

Opposite below: The Junkers Ju 88 was a versatile aircraft that was used in a wide range of wartime roles – from its use by Kampfgruppe (KG) 26 and KG 30 against the Arctic convoys, to the *Schräge-Musik*, upward-firing cannon-armed nightfighters defending the Reich. It had two main drawbacks: first, in the early days it was difficult to fly because it was so advanced; second, unlike many Allied aircraft, it was, as Andrew Brooke describes, 'designed with 4,000 different types of screw and bolt, and had to be riveted by hand'. Nevertheless, whether dropping 200 of the new SD-2 2kg 'butterfly bombs' that were devastating against aircraft on airfields or troops, or flying fast reconnaissance missions, the Ju 88 was the most important bomber in the Luftwaffe's inventory at the start of *Barbarossa* and continued throughout the war in the east to inflict heavy casualties to Soviet land and naval assets. This is likely Junkers Ju 88A-4 4D+GT of 9./KG 30 in the Balkans, May 1941.

Opposite above: The Junkers Ju 87 Stuka, with its gull wings and shrieking dive, is one of the classic images of Blitzkrieg. It was slow and could not carry a large bomb-load, and its vulnerability was shown up during the Battle of Britain. The Ju 87D-5 saw improved range, longer wings, two 20mm wing cannon and improved bomb-load from 500kg (1,100lb) of the Ju 87B to a maximum of 1,800kg (4,000lb) over short ranges – 1,200kg (2,600lb) being the usual, comprising a central fuselage 1,000kg bomb with 2 x 50kg bombs on each wing. The Ju 87G had a more specific anti-tank role, with two 37mm cannon mounted in underwing gunpods. They were limited in ammunition supply but the armour-piercing tungsten carbide rounds meant the Kanonenvogel ('cannon-bird') proved a serious tank-killer, the most famous proponent of this being Oberst Hans-Ulrich Rudel. This Ju 87D is armed with two 7.92mm MG 17 machine guns in wings and an MG 81 twin-barrel machine gun in the rear cockpit. Note the wing-mounted 50kg bombs.

Opposite below: The Focke-Wulf Fw 58 Weihe (Harrier), seen in the background of this off-duty moment, was a Luftwaffe trainer that could also be used for liaison, reconnaissance and ambulance duties. Over 1,600 were built and the main version – the 58C – was a six-passenger version.

Below: The Henschel Hs 126 was a reconnaissance and liaison aircraft that entered service with the Luftwaffe in 1939. Forty-seven Hs 126 squadrons took part in Operation *Barbarossa*. The plane was pulled from service in 1943 and replaced by the Fieseler Fi 156 Storch.

The Fieseler Fi 156 Storch (Stork) was also used as a reconnaissance and liaison aircraft and in German service from 1937 to 1945. Here a Storch is seen in Ukraine collecting Generaloberst Richard Ruoff – commander of 4. Panzerarmee from 8 January to 31 May 1942 – and Generaloberst Adolf Strauss, commander of 9. Armee until 14 January 1942. He was sacked following the German retreat in the face of the Soviet late 1941 counterattacks and failure of the *Taifun* attack on Moscow.

One of the Luftwaffe's major problems was its lack of transport aircraft. The mainstay of this role was the Junkers Ju 52/3m, which was obsolescent, slow and simply not built in sufficient quantities to fulfil the requirements – such as resupplying 6. Armee in surrounded Stalingrad. The Luftwaffe started the war with 552 Ju 52s, and around 2,800 were supplied between 1939 and 1945. Heavy losses meant that fewer than 200 of them were left at war's end. Note the open dorsal mounting for a 7.92mm MG 15, one of two carried for defence. It could tow two DFS 230 gliders, carry eighteen combat-ready troops, around 2,000kg (4,400lb) payload in its 16.7m$^3$ (590cu ft) cargo hold or 10 x 250kg containers. As a comparison, the C-47 could carry around 2,700kg (6,000lb). Almost the most important cargo for the Luftwaffe was fuel – particularly for the Panzers. For example, Renner calculates that on 12 July, during *Fall Blau*, the Luftwaffe delivered 200 cans of fuel to Panzer units. 488 Ju 52s were lost in the vain attempt to resupply the 6. Armee at Stalingrad when the paucity of Luftwaffe transport aircraft was made crucially plain. When used in the casualty evacuation role (inset), the craft could officially carry twelve stretchers.

2999

Only 200 of the Me 323 Gigant were built – a powered version of the Me 321 glider suggested by transport pilots who had flown the glider version on the Eastern Front. They may have been critically underpowered and with a very short range of around 1,100km (700 miles) when loaded, but they nevertheless fulfilled an important heavy transport function. They could carry around 12 tonnes – typical payloads were 130 men, 52 drums of fuel or an 8.8cm Flak gun and tractor – but needed rocket-assisted take-off to accomplish this. This one is seen in winter 1944 at Nikopol preparing to fly to the Crimea. These flights could not stop the German loss of the peninsula by 12 May 1944.

The Gotha Go 242B glider was an improvement on the DFS 230, although both were used through the war. It had a hinged rear door rather than the DFS 230's side door. Entering service in 1941, the Go 242B could carry twenty combat-ready troops. 1,500 were built, to be towed by He 111s, Ju 52s or Ju 87Ds. They were used by the Luftlandegeschwader (LLG) and Verbindungskommandos/Schleppgruppen (VK(S)/SG). LLG 2's Go 242Bs saw action on supply missions into the Velikiye Luki pocket at the end of 1942 and then the Kuban bridgehead from January to the end of March 1943 before moving west. Go 242B 614 is identified by the shield on its nose – a gull silhouetted against clouds with crossed sabres below – an emblem used by VK(S)4, which became SG2 in October 1943. VK(S)4 was formed in June 1942 at Nikolayev and flew missions supporting *Fall Blau*, the subsequent German retreat and the Kuban bridgehead. SG2 had two Gotha squadrons and supported troops in the Crimea and, after that became impossible, Hungary and Heeresgruppe Südukraine. The soldier in the foreground is well equipped for the cold weather. Unlike the army, Generalfeldmarschall Erhard Milch had made allowances for the Russian winter and ensured that there was adequate warm clothing and footwear for all 800,000 Luftwaffe personnel in the winter of 1941/42.

Between 1941 and 1945, combat with the Red Air Force accounted for 77,000 aircraft including air-to-air kills, aircraft downed by anti-aircraft guns and those destroyed on the ground from the air. In 1941 the Germans lost one aircraft per 25.5 sorties; in 1945 this was down to one in 11. A key factor was that the Luftwaffe just did not have enough aircraft and had to use their longer-range twin-engined bombers in close support of the army – something that led to heavy losses. This is the last resting place of a Focke-Wulfe Fw 189 Uhu (Owl) twin-boom reconnaissance aircraft. Over 850 of all versions of the so-called Fliegendes Auge (Flying Eye) were built.

# 3 On the Attack

THE WEHRMACHT PROVED ITSELF to be a superb fighting machine in attack in spite of its logistical problems. The massive encirclement battles of the Blitzkrieg years showed how German training, excellent leadership down to the lowest level and good-quality weaponry could be used to devastating effect. The Red Army could do little to cope with the aggression and tactical acumen shown by the Germans in the first months of *Barbarossa*.

The qualitative gap may have lessened as the war went on, but it was there right to the end. The Germans tried to simplify – MG 42 rather than MG 34, StuGs and Hetzer alongside Panther and Ferdinand – but failed. Too caught up in trying to produce the best weapon they could, they ended up losing the initiative to an army that went for functionality first and foremost. They may have won the qualitative war (although the number of big expensive tanks left on the side of the road because of lack of spare parts or engine problems militates against this) but they certainly lost the quantitative.

The German Army, for all its *Auftragstaktik* (mission command) and dashing Panzer leaders, also proved very set in its ways and incapable of tactical innovation. It always counterattacked when pushed off a position; its attacking option was almost always the *Keil und*

Left and opposite: They may not have achieved complete surprise – there had been intelligence that the Germans were coming – but on the day that Operation *Barbarossa* opened, the Soviet defences were wide open. Halder noted in his diaries, 'The enemy was surprised by the German attack. His forces were not in tactical disposition for defence. The troops in the border zone were widely scattered in their quarters. The frontier itself was for the most part weakly guarded.

'As a result of this tactical surprise, enemy resistance directly on the border was weak and disorganized, and we succeeded everywhere in seizing the bridges across the border rivers and in piercing the defense positions (field fortifications) near the frontier.'

*Kessel* encirclement battle. The Soviets learned from their failures and knew what to expect. And, whether by luck or judgement, at times they began to defuse *Keil und Kessel* by retreating before the *Kessel* (cauldron) could form. Soviet artillery was often able to stop counterattacks before they could take place.

German military intelligence was not always effective and became worse as the war went on, in large part because of the loss of air superiority. In the last two years of the war the Luftwaffe had so many problems that it was unable to supply suitable photographic reconnaissance. This was not helped by the fact that after late 1942 the Luftwaffe took control of photo reconnaissance from the army's commander of the air support (Koluft). A good example of the problems caused by poor intelligence is at Stalingrad, where the Germans thought the Soviets were on their last legs and missed the reserves massing for the counterattack.

Stalingrad also highlights the way that the Soviets innovated tactically by careful examination of their opponents. As Overy says,

> He [Marshal Vasily Chuikov] noted the German reliance on mass air and artillery attacks to push the infantry through, and the reluctance of German soldiers to engage in close combat without the protection of tanks. To reduce the impact of German firepower he insisted the two fronts should be no farther apart then 'the throw of a grenade'.

This reduced the effectiveness of the German bombers as the crews worried about hitting their own men. Chuikov added to this by pushing hand-to-hand combat and infiltration techniques to allow Soviet surprise attacks. The Germans were unable to answer the tactical questions this threw up.

'Air Force reports 850 enemy airplanes shot down. This number includes entire bomber squadrons committed without fighter escort, which were taken on and destroyed in the air by our fighters,' recorded Halder. The Luftwaffe played a crucial role in German offensive plans – on 22 June and all other occasions. Their morale was high at first until eroded by the interminable fighting and the losses. These Luftwaffe pilots (inset) are reliving combat in time-honoured style. One on one, they were often better than their Soviet opponents, but wartime attrition was considerable. Take Luftflotte 4's role during *Fall Blau* as an example. At the start it could mount over 10,000 sorties in a week. After eleven weeks of operations, the Luftflotte was down to 950 aircraft, of which only 550 were operational. This (right) is a Soviet Tupolev SB (ANT-40).

MADRID

The Germans did not have it all their own way after the initial weeks. As the war continued, the Red Air Force played a stronger and stronger role in the Soviet all-arms offence. Part of the reason for this was the reorganisation of the Red Air Force that took place in 1942 under a new leader, Alexander Alexandrovich Novikov. By the time of Stalingrad, the Red Air Force was able to halt the Luftwaffe and destroy over a thousand aircraft – including this Dornier Do 17Z-2, U5+GT *Madrid* of KG 2, which made a forced landing outside Demidov, north-west of Smolensk.

Time spent in reconnaissance ... Armoured car patrols were usually of three vehicles, with an artillery observer often accompanying the patrol so that covering fire could be brought down in an emergency. This type of patrol mission could last a couple of days. If the patrol came into contact with enemy forces, it avoided action unless the enemy was so weak it could be destroyed without diverting the patrol from its main mission. In some cases, if enemy action were likely, the patrol could be reinforced with SP guns and, sometimes, even tanks. Larger patrols could have engineers attached to deal with roadblocks and demolitions. Motorcyclists also played an important role.

The leichter Panzerspähwagen (SdKfz 222) was the Germans' standard light armoured car and was produced from 1936 replacing the earlier SdKfz 221. Armed with a 2cm KwK 30 (KwK 38 after 1942) autocannon and an MG 34, nearly a thousand of the three-man (commander, gunner, driver) vehicle were built. It had four-wheel drive but bogged easily; the range was poor, forcing the carriage of additional fuel drums; the turret was cramped and the armour too thin to be much protection – these limitations saw the SdKfz 250/9 take over the role later in the war. There were various series of SdKfz 222 built, the early ones identifiable (as here) by the older vision ports. The cage-like anti-grenade screens that protected the open-topped turret are open in this photograph.

Serial production of the eight-wheeled schwerer Panzerspähwagen started in 1937, taking over from the six-wheeled version that had been produced from 1932. The SdKfz 231 heavy armoured car was armed with a 2cm KwK 30 autocannon and a coaxial MG 34. Crewed by four men (driver, gunner, commander, wireless operator/second driver), it had two driving positions (front and rear) and improvements over its production run saw thicker armour and a better, more powerful, engine introduced. Note equipment stowage and, on the front, the angled stand-off armour that was added from 1940. This is from Panzer-Aufklarungs-Abteilung 5 of 5. Panzer-Division.

## The Armoured Spearhead

The key to any German offensive was the armoured spearhead. As Guderian put it, 'The Panzer regiment is the division's main strike force because of its firepower, armor and mobility.' The German Panzers developed swiftly in the 1930s and the force – four Panzergruppen totalling seventeen Panzer divisions plus vehicles held by the Heeresgruppen themselves – that entered the Soviet Union in 1941 was tried and tested (figures here and below from Operational Status Reports as shown in Thomas Jentz's book *Panzertruppen*).

HG Nord had Panzergruppe 4 and AOK Norwegen under command – three Panzer divisions for a total of 139 PzKpfw IIs, 155 PzKpfw 35(t)s, 118 PzKpfw 38(t)s, 71 PzKpfw IIIs, 80 PzKpfw IVs and 39 PzBefWg of various types, along with two battalions of tanks in Norway (some PzKpfw Is and IIs and French Beutepanzer).

Snow has not melted from the front of this schwerer Panzerspähwagen (Fu) SdKfz 232 – a variant of the 231 that had a bedstead aerial frame mounted on the roof (the wooden elements used to isolate the aerial are visible) This allowed reconnaissance troops to keep in contact up to 150km (90 miles) from HQ. Later in the war the bedstead aerial was replaced by the more discreet Sternantenne D. Note the *goldgelb Waffenfarbe* on the cap: after 1943 this was changed to the *rosarot* of the Panzer divisions.

HG Mitte had Panzergruppen 2 and 3 for a total of 144 PzKpfw Is, 393 PzKpfw IIs, 507 PzKpfw 38(t)s, 272 PzKpfw IIIs, 321 PzKpfw IVs and 89 PzBefWg of various types.

HG Süd had Panzergruppe 1 for a total of 8 PzKpfw Is, 211 PzKpfw IIs, 355 PzKpfw IIIs, 100 PzKpfw IVs and 54 PzBefWg of various types.

The armoured attack was hugely successful everywhere except in the far north, where intelligent Soviet defence – combined with too small an attacking force – ensured that Murmansk stayed Soviet, allowing a Lend–Lease pipeline of equipment, even though the convoys were hard hit by both Luftwaffe and Kriegsmarine, that would include 1,285 aircraft, 2,749 tanks, 81,287 machine guns, 26,500 tonnes (59,455,620lb) of explosives, along with food and clothing between October 1941 and June 1942.

The photographs that follow give a taste of the Panzers involved in *Barbarossa* and the years (1941–43) that saw the initiative with the German Army.

The PzKpfw I was obsolescent in 1941 and better used as a training vehicle; nevertheless there were a few Is and kleiner Befehlswagen in service for the attack, along with some 750 PzKpfw IIs (one of the latter is closest to the camera). Note the *dunkelgrau* colour of the vehicles, the vehicle identification numbers, the swastika on a red banner on the rear decking for IFF recognition, the tank assault badges on the two men nearest the camera and the WH/OT – Wehrmacht and Organization Todt – bumper marking of the bus.

Opposite above: Because of the delays encountered with the introduction of the PzKpfw III and IV into service – significant production of both only started in 1940 – the Czech armaments industry provided an excellent stopgap in the PzKpfw 35(t) and 38(t) (the t = *tschechisch* = Czech). They made up around a quarter of the more than 3,200 Panzers that attacked the Soviet Union. After being withdrawn from front-line service in late 1941/early 1942 they continued to see service in secondary roles or re-equipped with captured weapons as (amongst others) the Marder III, Grille, Flakpanzer 38 and Jagdpanzer 38 (later known as the Hetzer).

These PzKpfw 38(t)s are probably from 7. Panzer-Division (note the tactical marking on rear of sidecar) in winter 1941/42. The division started *Barbarossa* with 167 of them, fighting as part of Panzergruppe 3. They advanced through the major battles at Vyazma and Smolensk, finally advancing to gain a bridgehead over the Volga–Moscow Canal on 27 November 1941. It was the closest they got to the capital before being forced back. The division continued fighting until spring 1942, when it was sent to France to re-equip with PzKpfw IIIs and IVs. The riveted construction of the turret can be seen at right, and additional fuel tanks carried on the rear of the vehicles; trailers were also used.

Opposite below: The Germans were impressed by the Soviet T-34 and any they captured were used against their original owners. This one, with extensive German markings, is the subject of some interest as it is worked on in the Stalingrad area in 1942.

Above: Mobility, the Germans emphasised, was the key to tank warfare in attack and defence – and mobility does not necessarily mean speed. Postwar generations have become enamoured with the 'Top Trumps' approach to tank data, comparing armour thicknesses, gun maximum ranges and top speeds. In reality, few tanks moved at speeds greater than 16km/h (10mph) on anything less than good terrain – and at 25–32km/h (15–20mph) over the best surfaces, as these PzKpfw IIIs are enjoying. Wear and tear, combat conditions, mechanical issues all contributed to the reduction of mobility. The Germans proved adept at keeping their tanks on the road and handling many repairs at regimental level.

234

Above: 3. Panzer-Division was part of Panzergruppe 2 in Heeresgruppe Mitte. It went into *Barbarossa* with 13 PzKpfw Is, 58 PzKpfw IIs, 110 PzKpfw IIIs (of which 81 were armed with 5cm main guns), 32 PzKpfw IVs and 15 PzBefWgs. Attrition was a serious factor during the advance and by 4 September 1941, having had no replacements, these figures had eroded to: 5 PzKpfw Is, 30 PzKpfw IIs, 6 PzKpfw IIIs, 5 PzKpfw IVs and 8 PzBefWg operational vehicles. However, many had been deemed repairable so the actual total losses were reported as being 3 PzKpfw Is, 16 PzKpfw IIs, 35 PzKpfw IIIs, 12 PzKpfw IVs and 4 PzBefWgs (figures from Operational Status Reports in Jentz). The photo shows elements of the division entering Stary Bychów (today's Bychów) on the River Dnieper in Belarus.

Opposite above: Tank maintenance for men of 23. Panzer-Division. The Eiffel Tower emblem on the front left mudguard commemorates the fact that the division was formed around Paris. Note the lack of left-hand track and the hinged mudguard moved to enable work on the drive sprocket of this PzKpfw III Ausf L. To the left, the *Zeltbahn* tent has, as usual a helmet atop to stop rainwater entering through the join. Friedrich Sander mentioned maintenance in his diary: 'Just as commanders describe their days based on the action that happened, the drivers base their descriptions on the damage they had to repair. The day I describe as "the one on which Oswald finished off the big tank at Zvegiai", my driver describes as "the one on which my camouflage headlight was shot away". ... And for the old Skoda [Czech-built tanks, specifically in Sander's case, the PzKpfw 35(t)] drivers, these events are usually linked to the ever-increasing ailments of our "Skoda Super Sports". I hope we get rid of the old bangers soon. I stand in awe when I see the admirable and difficult work our maintenance and repair services are doing. The old Skodas in particular cause a huge amount of work.'

Opposite below: SS-Panzer-Abteilung 5 was the first of the Waffen-SS tank units and was originally intended for the *Das Reich* Division. Instead, in April 1942 it became part of the *Wiking* Division and served there until February 1943, when it became I. Abteilung of the newly formed SS-Panzer-Regiment 5. This PzKpfw III Ausf J, with its long-barrelled 5cm main gun, has the characteristic *Wiking* curved swastika. Note also the Ace of Spades to the right of the turret number.

Often touted as an example of the 'clean Waffen-SS', in fact *Wiking* was involved deeply with the Holocaust from the start. Lars Westerlunds writes of how Einsatzkommandos travelled with the division in 1942, helping to dispose of Jews and others. Soldiers of the division took part in these murderous activities right to the end of the division's war in Hungary in 1945.

The fighting was certainly not one-sided, as this photograph of a knocked-out PzKpfw III Ausf F at Bychów shows. Note that the open escape hatch that has been used by the wireless operator and the distinctive bear on the turret side. This identifies the vehicle as from I. /Panzer-Regiment 35 of 4. Panzer-Division. This *Abteilung* was nicknamed the *Bären Abteilung* (Bears Battalion) and each had a bear insignia. Jentz lists 4. Panzer's losses by 9 September 1941 as 2 PzKpfw Is, 17 PzKpfw IIs, 22 PzKpfw IIIs, 4 PzKpfw IVs and 5 PzBefWgs. Getting knocked out was not unusual and many crews survived, if not intact, then with casualties rather than deaths. After the crew bailed out, their first thought was often for their kit, as Sander related on 18 July 1941:

'"That's our tank burning there! They fired a few rounds right into it."

'"Damn! Has everyone managed to bail out?"

'"Yes, only it's tragic, all our stuff is still in there!"'

Above: The depth of the Russian winter came as a surprise to the Germans. It should not have done: there was plenty of information on the Arkhangelsk campaign of twenty or so years earlier, but the Wehrmacht had believed their own propaganda that the war would be over before the snows arrived. As Allen F. Chew writes, because of the extreme cold, 'the mechanisms of rifles and machine guns, and even the breechblocks of artillery, became absolutely rigid. The recoil liquid in artillery pieces also froze stiff, and tempered steel parts cracked. Strikers and striker springs broke like glass. ... [In] an encounter near Tikhvin when the temperature was -35°C (-31°F) only one of the five German tanks could fire.'

Below: PzKpfw III and IV in the snow. In 1941/42, short on cold-weather gear, the Germans were forced to find shelter to survive – and that meant villages. They simply could not maintain lines out in the open without suffering huge numbers of cold-weather injuries. Control, therefore, of these vital points became the focus of fighting – and if retreat was necessary, the villages were torched so the enemy could not use them. Sander noted on 9 December 1941: 'Yesterday we were morally defeated, just like Napoleon's victorious troops were. We were forced to retreat. We, the former Panzer men, had been sent ... to cover our retreat and to torch villages! Yes, we have turned into proper murderous arsonists.'

In the freezing conditions the Germans had continuous problems with their artillery and heavy weapons, and motor vehicles, including the tanks. Starting when frozen was particularly difficult. They tried tow-starting but this damaged motors and differentials and was not easy for heavy armour. In the end, keeping the engines heated with a fire underneath the vehicle or simply letting them run for hours were the only ways to survive.

912

Above: The long-barrelled 14.5mm anti-tank rifles used by the Soviets proved remarkably effective against the thinner side armour and vision ports of such German tanks as the PzKpfw III, IV and even the Panther. Used in quantity, they were enough of a threat for the Germans to come up with a solution: *Schürzen* – side skirts. They were introduced on the PzKpfw IV Ausf G in spring 1943 and used to the end of the war, later versions being the wire-mesh 'Thoma-Schilden' – probably named after Generalinspekteur der Panzertruppen Generaloberst Heinz Guderian's chief of staff, General Wolfgang Thomale. Wartime photographs show that the 5cm-thick plates were often incomplete. Note the camouflage: *dunkelgelb* with *olivgrün* overlay.

Opposite above: Don't try this at home! Tanks dislike extreme temperatures and Panzer-Abteilung 211's Hotchkiss tanks were no exception. Over 500 of the French light tanks fell into German hands in 1940 and they were employed as PzKpfw 35H 734(f) or 38H 735(f). Many methods were employed to cope with the cold, including using fires under the engine to thaw it out. One of two units that fought in Finland, Panzer-Abteilung 211 was unusual in that, until 1944, it was equipped completely with Beutepanzer: ex-French Army Somua S-35s and, as here, Hotchkiss H-39s.

Opposite below: Turret number 912, a 22. Panzer-Division PzKpfw IV Ausf F2 or early G with 7.5cm KwK 40 L/43 main gun, is pictured in the Crimea. Note the camouflage scheme of *dunkelgelb* and *olivgrün*, the red of the flag draped over the turret rear – for recognition by the Luftwaffe – and the MG 34 infantry squad on the rear decking. Modellers should note the way that mud collects on the road wheels and driving sprocket. In the background is a SdKfz 251/3 or 6 with a frame aerial, hiding in the lee of a building – perfect for a modelling diorama.

22. Panzer-Division had an unenviable history. Introduced into action on a foggy 20 March 1942 against a Soviet offensive, it suffered accordingly. Pulled out of action only a matter of hours later, the division had lost nearly a quarter of its strength – mainly PzKpfw 38(t)s. It suffered a similar debacle in November 1942 during the Soviet Operation *Uranus* and was subsequently disbanded.

What looks like a brand-new factory-delivered PzKpfw IV Ausf G is being prepared for service. Note lack of Panzer black and the overalls on the man passing ammunition into the tank; brass shell cases can be seen beside his feet. The weapons are covered to keep them clean and there are a lot of boxes and containers scattered around. In the photo we can see the *dunkelgelb* overall paint scheme, the lack of loader's vision ports on the side and front of the turret (eliminated on the Ausf G) and the double hatch cover on the commander's cupola. Later in the run this was changed to a new cupola with a single-piece hatch and *Schürzen* were included.

The Ausf F1 was the last of the PzKpfw IV series to mount a short KwK 37 L/24 7.5cm main gun. Thereafter the longer KwK 40 L/43 or L/48 was employed. The Ausf F1 was the first to incorporate the double doors on the turret sides, one with a vision port and the other with a pistol port. This is very evident on the tank in the background. Also visible is the wireless aerial deflector under the main gun, to ensure that the coaxial machine gun did not damage the aerial. It had non-conductive material attached to the bottom so that it did not affect signal. Some long 7.5cm gun tanks had a similar deflector but this was obviated in later models by moving the aerial to the left rear.

Above: In the attack, especially in the first months of *Barbarossa*, there was little soul-searching. Friedrich Sander knew exactly what he thought about it: 'Every soldier on our side knows what the great objective of all this is. And not only that, they have all grasped the deeper sense of it.

'There, just look at it! All that rich soil and there are acres and acres of it. But it's all so badly cultivated! In this country we feel like the Goths and Vandals once did, when they migrated from their overcrowded lands and, weapon in hand, sought new soil for themselves! If these people here are incapable of cultivating the land, then they have no claim on it! Just look at the sheep and goats, so squalid and ill-bred. Bring German settlers here! They know about cultivation and animal breeding.'

Others, however, were less interested in the Lebensraum, Sanders again: 'The average Landser though is looking forward to more mundane things. Every Landser in my platoon has by now asked me: "There will surely be schnapps factories in Leningrad, Herr Leutnant?"'

Here a PzKpfw IV towing a fuel trailer heads towards the start line for *Barbarossa*.

Below: Soviet artillery was a powerful tool against any attacks, and as the war continued, so the Red Army began to use its artillery in a more coordinated fashion. The US War Department, in *Soviet Field Artillery in the Offensive,* reported that the July 1943 battle for Orel 'was the greatest artillery duel and the most prolonged battle of the war up to that time. Maximum accuracy of fire was required and was attained. One month was spent in developing this accuracy, using every conceivable method to locate enemy batteries, alternate firing positions, personnel shelters, approaches, etc. Calculations of coordinates of enemy installations were based upon acoustic intersections, surveys, and aerial photographs, constantly corrected by observation. The fire plan was so completely integrated that every gun had specific targets and fired only at those targets.' This 22. Panzer-Division PzKpfw IV has been ravaged by Soviet artillery. The division was destroyed on the River Chir in late 1942.

WH 406735

Left: The initiative passed from the Germans to the Soviets during 1943. While the loss of 6. Armee at Stalingrad may have been the moment the Germans should have realised that and acted accordingly; instead they launched one more massive assault on the now revitalised Red Army. Worse than that, the attack was telegraphed. The Soviets knew where it was coming and prepared for it. Perhaps the best example of how badly the Germans mangled their last strategic attempt to crush the Red Army is the way that their new tank, the PzKpfw V Panther, was rushed into action, the attack being delayed until it was ready. Apart from the teething problems that saw automotive unreliability reduce the number of operative Panthers from 200 to 40 inside two days, the tanks were also delivered without sufficient crew training, radio checks or any field reconnaissance or familiarisation with the terrain. The result was a catastrophe. By 20 July, 41 were operational, 85 under repair/repairable in theatre, 16 under repair/repairable in Germany, 56 irreparable (enemy action) and 2 irreparable (engine fires). There was a plus point: they claimed 267 enemy tanks knocked out. The gun and its accuracy at distance was confirmed.

Opposite: Designed as an infantry support vehicle, the early marks of Sturmgeschütz were based on the PzKpfw III chassis and armed with a 7.5cm StuK 37 L/24 main gun. Their role was to provide the infantry with a weapon that could destroy enemy strongpoints and heavy weapons. It was to have a low silhouette and was designed to shoot from a stationary position always with close infantry protection. A key point: the StuGs were not tanks and the crew did not wear Panzer black. They were designated part of artillery, their *Waffenfarbe* was red and they wore a green-grey version of the Panzer jacket. The Ausf A entered service in February 1940 and the Ausf E at the end of 1941. By July 1942, 619 StuGs were ready for action. The Ausf E is distinguished by the armoured panniers along the sides of the superstructure. This excellent photograph shows a command vehicle of Sturmgeschütz-Abteilung 197 of 22. Panzer-Division in the Crimea. Note the camouflage roughly applied over the *dunkelgrau* of the StuG and the staff car. Sturmgeschütz-Abteilung 197 went on to become schwere Panzerjäger Abteilung 653 equipped with Ferdinands.

On 24 May 1945, at the Seventh Army Interrogation Center, PoW German generals Guderian, von Geyr, Dietrich, Hausser and others were quizzed about German tank losses. Alex Coox et al's *Survey of Tank Losses* summarised their estimates. Most of the generals felt that mechanical failures or terrain were the main causes (Guderian thought they were responsible for 60–70 per cent of the losses; Dietrich and Hausser less). Guderian attributed 15 per cent of losses to A/T; 5 per cent to artillery; 5 per cent to mines; and 5 per cent to other causes. It is surprising that they did not see mines as more of a problem. The Soviet records claim 222 million mines laid in the Second World War, many of these in their rear areas, Soviet engineers infiltrating German lines and targeting heavily trafficked roads, railroads, airfields and communication centres. They were laid on road shoulders, in ditches and side roads. It is difficult to identify the cause of the demise of this StuG III Ausf E at Kherson, but artillery would be a good bet.

The StuG III Ausf G, otherwise known as the StuG 40 Ausf G, was the most-produced version of the assault gun. Produced from December 1942 and armed with a 7.5cm StuK L/48 main gun, around 8,400 were constructed by Alkett and MIAG. It is identifiable by the slanted ends to the side panniers. Some later vehicles had the distinctive *Saukopf* (sow's head) mantlet. The upgunning had started with the Ausf F, and the extra hitting power helped the StuG become an excellent tank destroyer – so much so that Guderian, when he became Inspector General of the Armoured Forces, did his best to have the Sturmartillerie and Panzerjäger amalgamated. Debogging tracked vehicles from mud was an occupational hazard for crews and Panzer engineers. Suitable prime movers were essential as recovery vehicles to keep the Panzerwaffe on the move – as here (below)

Another one bites the dust. Nearly 45,000 Soviet medium tanks (mainly T-34s) were knocked out during the war. Soviet total losses were staggering – nearly 100,000 (Grigori Krivosheev and Alexandr Kruglov identify the figure as 5,200 heavy, 44,900 medium, 33,500 light and 13,000 SP guns). The Germans lost around 24,000 (Burkhart Müller-Hillebrand cites the figure of 15,700 tanks, 5,200 StuGs and 3,000 SP guns).

However, it is worth pointing out that these figures (a) do not only cover combat; (b) that German vehicles were more often repaired and put back into service than Red Army ones; and (c) many of the Soviet losses in 1941 were from the initial invasion.

A knocked-out KV-1 near Stalingrad in 1942. It was photographed by a 297. Infanterie-Division soldier. Part of Heeresgruppe Süd, the division fought at Kiev in 1941 and was involved in the retaking of Kharkov in 1942. It fought under 6. Armee and was destroyed at Stalingrad. When the Germans first came across the KV-1 heavy tank, their shells bounced off it. It needed 8.8cm guns or close combat and the use of satchel charges to destroy one. However, the tank was extremely heavy and unmanoeuvrable and consequently lacked mobility. The lighter variant, the KV-1S, was an improvement but not sufficient to lead to continued production after the T-34 was upgraded. The KV-1 was replaced later in the war by the Joe Stalin tanks (Kliment Voroshilov having fallen from grace!). By that time, the Germans had come up with a range of heavier tanks and guns that could compete with the KV series. The losses sustained by the Soviet tank formations in 1941 and 1942 beggar belief. Many of them fell victim to tanks that were less potent but better used. Training, good commanders, honed tactics and, often, surprise all helped the German Panzerwaffe. The Soviets caught up, but they lost many brave men in the process.

Inset: The glacis of a Red Army T-34, also photographed by a 297. Infanterie-Division soldier, near Stalingrad in 1942. It has received a critical blow. Note the rough welding, the hull Degtyaryov DP 7.62mm machine gun and the opening of the driver's hatch. The T-34 was the key element in the Soviet armoured forces. Introduced in 1940, it had many manufacturing defects, problems which meant that it was hard to use tactically: no radio except in commanders' vehicles, a cramped turret in which the commander was also the gunner, plus poor vision devices. But it improved over the course of the war – and over 57,000 examples, 22,000 of which were the improved T-34/85 – as did Soviet tank tactics, crews and gunnery. By 1945, some of the units were as good as anything the Germans had.

## River Crossings

The German advance across the Soviet Union had to overcome numerous river obstacles. It soon became obvious that key issues were engineer reconnaissance – finding the best places to cross either by rebuilding destroyed bridges or replacing them (an important factor here was to ensure the bridges could cater for heavy armour because many Soviet bridges were unsuitable) – strong engineer forces incorporated in advance detachments so they could start working quickly and not allow the bridge building to hold up the advance; and sufficient forces and air cover to protect from enemy attempts to negate the bridgehead. Friedrich Sander noted in his diary: 'But now there is no more going forward because ahead the Russians have blown up the bridge across the piss-filled ditch in front of Dubrova. The brothers finally seem to have discovered how they can stop a gang like ours. But never mind, pioneers have already rolled to the front, where they have to build a new bridge. The wooden frames they call bridges here are usually so badly built that they can hardly carry the weight of a Panzer IV anyway. Virtually all of them need reinforcing.'

The main German bridging units, the Brückenkolonnen (BrKol), carried equipment that could make either bridges or ferries. Brückenkolonne A, for example, was a throwback to the First World War and the Reichswehr. It could create 3-tonne, 4-tonne and 7-tonne ferries; BrKol B could make a number of 4-tonne/8-tonne double/8-tonne simple/16-tonne ferries; BrKol C was lighter and constructed ferries up to 4 tonnes; BrKol D carried material for reconnaissance units; BrKol G was for mountain troops and BrKol I for heavier loads. Bridging units were also taken from Austrian and Czech forces.

Above: Trusting the original Soviet bridges could be a mistake, although some or the ersatz corduroy jobs put up by the German engineers looked dodgy. Certainly, some passengers of this 19. Panzer-Division SdKfz 6 seem to be keeping a watchful eye on the progress of the 8.8cm gun as it crosses a stream near Minsk. Part of Panzergruppe 3, 19. Panzer spent most of its war on the Eastern Front save for a two-month period in May–July 1944 when it was in the Netherlands.

Opposite: Another 3. Panzer-Division photograph, this one taken on 1 July 1941 as Panzer-Regiment 6 crossed the River Beresina, a tributary of the Dnieper east of Minsk. From here, Panzergruppen 2 and 3 headed across the Dnieper itself towards the great encirclement battle of Smolensk. The bridge here – a 16-tonne bridge – was erected using Brückenkolonne B: large pontoons carried in halves on Pf 11 wagons pulled by trucks such as the Henschel Type 33. The two platoons of such a column carried sufficient material to build an 83m (270ft) 8-tonne bridge or a 54m (180ft) 16-tonne bridge.

The River Don is a significant river by anyone's standards and its easterly bend takes it to within 60km (37 miles) of the Volga and Stalingrad. Von Paulus attacked across the river on 21 August 1942 and took the Soviets by surprise, enabling LI. Korps to create a bridgehead 5km (3 miles) by 8km (5 miles). The German engineers hurried to take advantage and erected bridges at Vertyachiy big enough to allow XIV. Panzerkorps to cross. On 23 August with the aerial support of VIII. Fliegerkorps, XIV Panzerkorps attacked towards the Volga. By the 30th, they were knocking on Stalingrad's front door.

Ferries were used extensively, this one from planks stretched over rubber boats was sufficient to carry motorcycles and crews. Note the *G* (= *Guderian* = Panzergruppe 2) on the rear of the sidecar next to the tactical symbol for 3. Panzer-Division, one of five divisions in the Panzergruppe.

## Infantry in the Attack

The German infantry squad was built around the squad machine gun: initially an MG 34, latterly an MG 42. The MG 34 had a maximum rate of fire of 1,000 rounds a minute but there are few occasions when a gunner would have been so profligate. Controlled bursts at 200–500 rounds was more usual – barrels heated up with heavy use and necessitated barrel changes. The gunner had an assistant and an ammunition carrier, but in practice most of the squad – the squad leader and six riflemen – would carry ammo.

'What are your orders, sir?' An Oberst (in crusher cap) and his HQ. From the start, officers were trained to rely on their own judgement. *Auftragstaktik* – mission-led tactics – was the key to superior German leadership. This meant that junior officers had the flexibility to determine the best means of fulfilling their mission and not rigidly following orders.

A PzKpfw II is visible in the background.

Infantrymen are an essential part of armoured warfare. Tanks rarely operate without infantry protection; if they do, they often fall victim to enemy infantry weapons. As the Germans trained for war, they knew they needed all arms together with high mobility to give the attack weight and speed. But how to move the infantry? What was needed was a vehicle that could keep pace with tanks, could move across country as they did and could protect the troops within. Halftracks were a good solution: already in use as prime movers, all they needed was a suitable armoured body. And thus the Schützenpanzerwagen – SPW – was born. The first was the leichter (light) SPW, SdKfz 251, based on the SdKfz 11 prime mover body (over 6,600 were produced during the war). They proved successful: cheaper to produce than tanks, the army thought they would work in the reconnaissance role carrying a Halbgruppe (half platoon). This led to the mittlerer (medium) SPW, SdKfz 250, based on the SdKfz 10 prime mover's chassis (over 15,000 produced). There were many variants of each type, with various weaponry. This is one of 16. Panzer-Division's SdKfz 251 mSPW (Wurfrahmen 40), which could carry six (three on each side) 28cm or 32cm Wurfrahmen 40 rockets.

16. Panzer-Division in Ukraine in summer 1942 during *Fall Blau*, showing a wide variety of vehicles: tanks, armoured vehicles, cars and motorcycles. The division fought in the great encirclement battle at Kiev but was destroyed at Stalingrad.

The SdKfz 8 was a 12-ton heavy prime mover made in a number of versions, DBs7–8 and DB9–10, from 1934 to 1944. The difference between the DBs8 and DB9 was the type of engine, so it is difficult to identify them visually. Over 200 of these types were built, out of a total of over 4,000. The tow load improved from 12 tonnes to 14 tonnes with the DB10. The heaviest halftrack the Wehrmacht had when it entered service, the SdKfz 8 lost that crown when the 18-ton SdKfz 9, the Famo, arrived in 1938. This DBs8 or 9 has burnt out: halftracks were always very vulnerable to air attack.

Above: Field maintenance was crucially important to keep the German advance going. Military vehicles undergo significant wear and tear – especially if they are motoring from the Polish border into the Caucasus – and, where possible, much of the day-to-day workload was handled by the crews. Here an SdKfz 7 spring suspension is worked on, the wood is being used to hold the track out of the way. The 8-ton halftrack was used as a recovery vehicle.

Opposite above: The 19. Panzer-Division's order of battle, described by George Nafziger, identifies a range of nominally available artillery in June 1942 when this photograph was taken – including the 15cm sIGs of the motorised infantry gun companies and the heavy weapons of the 19. Panzer-Artillerie-Regiment (18 x 10.5cm leFH 18, 3 x 10cm K18, 3 x 15cm sFH 18). The sFH 18 heavy howitzer was well liked by the German Army. It had a split-trail carriage, launched a 44kg shell and had a travelling weight of 6,300kg – only a third of the weight of the 15cm Kanone 18. It was important that artillery kept up with the armour to negate counterattacks and for counterbattery work, but even with its lesser weight, most of the time the sFH 18 still had to travel at the rate it could be dragged by horses. Its main problem, however, was that its range was not as good as its Soviet equivalent, the 152mm ML-20, which could subject the German guns to counterbattery fire with a 4km (2.5-mile) leeway. The Germans attempted to bridge this gap with the 18M model that had used increased charge sizes, a barrel liner and a muzzle brake. The 18M did not prove successful, so the next option was a rocket-assisted round, which certainly improved the range.

Opposite below: Mortars were extremely important in the attack and were heavily used by both sides on the Eastern Front. The German Army initially used two of them: the light 5cm Granatwerfer 36 and the heavy 8cm GrW 34. The GrW 34's crew of four or five (two crews are seen here) carry the three segments and ammunition. Panzergrenadiere used the GrW 34 mortars in halftracks (the SdKfz 250/7 and 251/2). During the war, the Germans realised that they needed to emulate the Soviets and use heavier mortars – 10.5cm and 12cm weapons were introduced.

Above: The biggest problem with German artillery was its dependence on horses to draw it. Motorised artillery units not only moved faster, but they required fewer people to crew the weapons. Most German artillery could be towed by vehicles although this usually necessitated rubber tyres, some springing of equipment and differently designed trailers. The main artillery prime movers were the SdKfz 6 to 11 halftracks, this one being an SdKfz 8 towing a 15cm sFH 18 heavy howitzer and having plenty of room for its seven-man crew.

Opposite above: Yes, it's trite, but an army really does march on its stomach. Food is more important than most niceties in the field and on the way to the front. The German Army, of course, had a range of cooking vehicles from bread dough mixer trailer (the SdAh 35), various bakery trailers (SdAh 105 and 106) and a range of kitchen trailers, including the small (Hf 12 and its improved 14 version) and large (Hf 11 and 13) field kitchens. This one is a grosse Feldküche (large field kitchen). Note behind the cooks the *Essenträger* hot water-filled double-skinned containers that were used to ferry the hot food rations to the troops.

Opposite below: Sander recounted: 'At 16.00 our artillery opened fire on the edge of the village ahead of us to suppress enemy anti-tank guns. At the same time we followed the advance of our infantry, overtaking them before exiting the village. The artillery then shifted its fire further into the forest ahead. It all went smoothly in a textbook manner.' Artillery plays a major role in any offensive, both to soften up an enemy in preparation for the attack (with the drawback being that this identifies the point of attack) and to neutralise defenders by suppressing fire that keeps their heads down, allowing the attack time to close to the enemy. With artillery observers riding with the armoured brigade, an armoured division's artillery can be on hand to lay down intense fire support as attacks go in. The artillery then concentrates on counterbattery fire against the defenders' artillery, and harassing fire against anti-tank units and observation posts. Artillery is also important to protect flanks created by a tank attack. The Germans had a good selection of weapons including the 10.5cm leFH 18 (leichte Feldhaubitze = light field howitzer) seen here. Over 20,000 of this and two developments, the leFH 18M (also used on the Wespe) and leFH 18/40 (a lighter version that entered service in 1943), were built and the weapon proved adaptable in the field. It was also used in the anti-tank role.

Some 830 Renault R35s were taken by the Germans when the fighting in France stopped. Many were later used – as here – as artillery tractors after having had the turret removed. (Some of the turrets were used on Tobruks.) In this form it was identified as the Artillerieschlepper 35R(f). This one is pulling a heavyweight: the carriage of the 21cm Mörser 18. It could fire a 110kg (250lb) shell out to 14.5km (9 miles). The barrel was carried separately.

The SdKfz 2 Kettenkrad (full title kleines Kettenkrad HK101) was a halftrack with a motorcycle front wheel and saw extensive use in many roles on the Eastern Front. Here one is towing a 7.5cm PaK 97/38 which married a French 75mm M1897, a Solothurn muzzle brake and a 5cm PaK 38 carriage. There were over 3,700 of the resulting weapon produced in 1942–43. It was known for its heavy recoil.

## Portrait of the Enemy: The Red Army

Purged of its senior officers in 1936–39, the Red Army undertook a massive expansion in the runup to war. The reorganisation was still underway in October 1940 when more senior officers were executed. As a result of the disorder and lack of experience, the Red Army was in no shape to resist the powerful thrusts of an experienced, battle-hardened force when the Germans invaded. The results were spectacularly bad for the Soviets (which occasioned even more purges), with defeat after defeat, leading to over 3 million Red Army soldiers becoming PoWs and the German Army reaching the outskirts of Moscow.

Four years later, Soviet tanks stood next to the Brandenburger Tor, the Hammer and Sickle flew above the Reichstag and the Führer's half-burnt body lay in a shallow grave outside the Reichskanzlei. How had the Red Army managed this remarkable turnaround?

While the Soviet successes were in part down to German mistakes and arrogance, in large part they were down to the sacrifice, dogged resourcefulness and ability to learn shown by the men and women of the Red Army. In spite of huge casualties, time and again they stood, fought and died in battle against the invading army. They did so because they knew the alternative was extinction. They could see what the Germans did to their country and families when they took ground. They could also see – thanks to Order No. 227 – what would happen if they did try to run.

Then the tide turned and between June 1944 and May 1945 the Red Army advanced from the Dnieper to Berlin. Operation *Bagration* epitomises the improvements the Soviets

The Nazis in general, and Adolf Hitler in particular, thought that the people of the Soviet Union were *Untermenschen*, and they expected a short war. Matthew Cooper quotes General Alfred Jodl, OKW Chief of Operations, speaking for the German High Command when he said, 'the Russian colossus will be proved to be a pig's bladder; prick it, and it will burst.' Friedrich Sander knew that was wrong when he noted in his diary: 'The Russian is an opponent who has been clearly underestimated by our politicians!' This Russian PoW still has most of his equipment – probably not for long. Note the puttees, the rolled greatcoat, long *gimnasterka* tunic, breeches, plain enlisted man's belt and *pilotka* side cap. Unless he is lucky enough to become a Hiwi, there is a good chance he'll die of starvation on the march to a camp or be shot dead while trying to forage for food. If he makes it to the camp, and if he does not succumb to disease, he may well be worked to death as a slave labourer. Of the 5.7 million Soviet PoWs recorded (and many died before they could be recorded) more than 3.5 million died in captivity.

had made. They camouflaged the point of attack brilliantly, destroyed HG Mitte and advanced to the Vistula. The Germans never recovered from the loss of half a million casualties.

Our view of the Red Army is undoubtedly coloured by the Cold War. As the Soviet Union became the West's adversary, so West Germany was needed as part of NATO. With the Soviet archives closed, the Eastern Front battles were dissected by German generals with their own agendas. They blamed their defeat on Soviet numbers, the mad strategy of Hitler, the weather – almost anything other than the prowess of the Red Army, although it was difficult to hide the fact that between 1941 and 1945 the Soviets had destroyed some 607 Axis divisions.

Some 900,000 women served in the Red Army. While many were employed in the same sort of roles as in other armies (hospital staff, communications, admin), there were many who fought – as infantry, in tanks and aircraft; even as snipers. Those who were captured were often shot out of hand. This was sanctioned at the highest level. Franka Maubach writes that Generalfeldmarschall Günther von Kluge, commander of 4. Armee, issued an order, illegal and later rescinded, that all captured Soviet female soldiers were to be shot. Many Germans found it difficult to believe that women actually fought on the front line. It goes without saying that many were raped – if not at the front, then more often than not by rear-echelon troops, Hiwis and auxiliaries. Others renounced their PoW status and were sent to civilian forced labour programmes. The woman in this photograph is wearing a *gimnasterka* tunic.

PoWs being interrogated. The heavy MG is a Pulemyot Maxima PM1910/30 (the long-lived Maxim MG), a 7.62mm belt-fed, water-cooled, wheel-mounted heavy MG with an armoured shield. This devastating weapon needed a team of four to six. Note the steel ammunition cases in front of it; each holds a canvas belt of 250 rounds. The Wehrmacht had been told that the rules did not apply to Soviet PoWs. Friedrich Sander noted in his diary on 19 July 1941: 'Two more men in civilian dress are brought up, they had tried to set fire to a captured petrol storage and in the process had fired on our men. Flak-Leutnant Sander's question about what to do with the pigs is met with a short reply by an Adjutant on the General's staff: "Shoot them!" The two are led behind a house, a few minutes later a few pistol shots can be heard. Done – sorted, a couple fewer fanatical Bolsheviks.'

Above: In the foreground, a Soviet BA-10 (BA = Broneavtomobil = armoured car). This 6 x 4 heavy armoured car weighed in at 5,140kg (5.7 tons). With a crew of four (commander, driver, gunner and machine-gunner), it supported infantry with its 45mm 20-K high-velocity gun as well as performing as a reconnaissance vehicle. It could be converted to a halftrack to improve its offroad manoeuvrability by using easily attached track belts. By 1942 it had been replaced by the T-60 and T-70 light tanks. In the middle distance is a Soviet T-26 light tank and a 94. Infanterie-Division lorry.

Opposite: On the other side of the coin from the T-34, the Soviet T-35(A) was an ungainly behemoth weighing around 54 tonnes. It had five turrets – the main one had a 75mm KT-28 gun with a coaxial DT (Degtyaryova Tankovy) 7.62mm machine gun; the two at the front carried a 45mm 20-K gun (on the right) and the other a DT; so did the two at the rear, with the weapons swapping sides. The T-35 was slow and unreliable, and during *Barbarossa* more were lost to mechanical problems than enemy action. The photo shows the improved T-35(A) with sloped armour on the turrets and newly modified side skirts. It had ten crew: commander, gunner and loader in the main turret, two manning each 45mm gun, one in each MG turret and a driver. Of the sixty or so built, there were only ten of this sloped turret armour version.

The T-26 was very much a tank of its time. It was excellent in the interwar period, when it was produced in greater numbers than any other tank. By 1941 it was obsolete and less of a match for the German PzKpfw III and IV tanks, although still better armed than the PzKpfw Is and IIs and the Czech PzKpfw 35(t) and 38(t) tanks in German service which made up as much as 45 per cent of the German Panzers for *Barbarossa*. When in good condition and with a good crew – something of a rarity – the T-26 gave a good account of itself. Loosely based on the British Vickers 6-ton Type B, from 1933 the T-26 had a Soviet-designed turret mounting a high-velocity 45mm 19-K gun and a coaxial DT MG, as seen in these photographs of T-26s knocked out near Smolensk. The T-26 was the main tank to oppose the German onslaught, although of the 10,000 in the Soviet inventory many were not operational due to automotive and other problems. They continued in Soviet service throughout the war.

Another design that was obsolete by 1941, the medium T-28 tank was a smaller and lighter version of the T-35 multi-turreted heavy tank. Both suffered from automotive issues, lack of spares and poor maintenance. The main gun on the T-28 was a decent 76.2mm howitzer, with four DT MGs, including two in separate forward-mounted small turrets, obscured by the misplaced main turret in this photograph. The 400 or so still in service in 1941 played little part in the war after the first disastrous months, having succumbed to automotive troubles or swifter German vehicles.

The T-40 was a two-man amphibious light tank primarily intended for reconnaissance. The offset, welded, conical turret held its main armament – a 0.50in (12.7mm) DShK MG. The boat-shaped hull was entirely welded for obvious reasons and replaced earlier models which relied on attached pontoons. Propulsion in

water was by a well-protected hull propeller and rudder. The chassis was used in simplified form for the T-60 light tank, of which some 6,000 were made. The T-40 was discontinued and most were lost in the first six months of the war. This one burnt out in Bohushivka, Ukraine.

The much-vaunted T-34 medium tank is usually cited as being the reason for the Panther. The Germans were, apparently, shocked by it. Certainly, the Soviets had learned the lessons from the Mongolian Campaign where its early predecessor, the petrol-fuelled T-26, was found to be vulnerable and inadequate. The first T-34s appeared in September 1940 and they were destined to replace the T-26, BT series (Christie suspension) and the T-28. However, the T-34 had problems. The turret was cramped and the commander also acted as gunner. There were quality issues as production became erratic when the factories were moved to the Urals to escape the advancing Germans; for example there was poor welding (the tanks leaked badly in wet weather). These

issues were not addressed because quantity became paramount the nearer the Axis got to Stalingrad. The Dzerzhinsk tractor factory continued production as fighting raged until it was forced to move production out of the city. Losses of the T-34s were staggering but as the Germans were pushed back, production increased and the faults were rectified. A new three-man turret, an improved gun and better construction and armour made a significant difference. This vehicle has the smaller two-man turret. It and the hull have been penetrated and shots through the front mudguard have broken the track. The photo was taken by a man from 9. Infanterie-Division after the Battle of Brody.

Another photograph showing the aftermath of the Battle of Brody, late June 1941. The battle typified the problems that the Soviets faced and obscured German deficiencies. Lack of adequate communications, poor coordination (or none) between units, mechanical breakdowns on a massive scale before any contact, lack of fuel and ammunition, inadequate air support, poor coordination with other arms, artillery in particular – the Soviets fought in an uncoordinated manner and the Germans took advantage with their obsolete Czech and early Panzers. Soviet tank losses vary from source to source but could be as high as 2,500, although most were the old and obsolete T-26, T-28 and BT-7. It is unclear why these T-34s are in the River Dubno. The bridge does not look robust enough to take their weight, so was it a rash attempt to cross the water? Alternatively, as one Soviet commentator suggests, when ammunition and fuel ran out, the tank crews drove their tanks into the river to make it more difficult for the Germans to retrieve them – because the Germans would have retrieved them if possible. The tanks would then have been redesignated and put to use against their previous owners.

The BT-7 light tank (BT = *Bystrokhodny tank* = high-speed tank) was fast and manoeuvrable and derived from the US Christie tank. It had a crew of three, a 45mm 20-K gun and a coaxial DT machine gun in the two-hatch turret. This Model 1937 has a DT MG mounted on an AA turret mount. These tanks suffered huge losses in the early days of *Barbarossa* through battle or mechanical failure.

Inset: The KV-2 heavy artillery tank was armed with a 152mm M-10T howitzer in its big turret and was designed as a bunker-buster. With a crew of six, difficult to steer, a turret that was a challenge to traverse and at 52 tonnes, it was too heavy and expensive to produce, so only about 210 were built.

The KV-2 was too slow for a mobile war, and while its armour was impenetrable to German anti-tank weapons, infantry could destroy it from the rear – sometimes with the simple expedient of jerrycans of fuel. Air power, especially the Henschel Hs 129 with its high-velocity 30mm cannon, also proved deadly. In front of the KV-2 is a captured British 15cwt 4 x 2 Morris Commercial with aircraft recognition panel.

The KV-1 heavy tank (inset) proved well armoured and the Germans had problems penetrating it in 1941. Over 5,000 were built, but by 1942 its armour provided insufficient protection against the more modern German anti-tank guns. It is difficult to see the different shades of Soviet tank camouflage from burnt-out models, but they did exist, although rarely. From the start of the 1940s the basic colour was dark green, 4BO. Most vehicles reached the front line in this colour. It was occasionally varied with dark brown (6K) and green black (7K) in a two- or three-colour scheme – although this was fairly rare until the end of 1941 when the green black was changed to yellow (7K). Snow camouflage involved white paint with green if the fighting was not out in the open. And, of course, foliage was used – the Soviets thought this more important than multiple-colour camouflage.

Camouflage colours are visible on this Model 1939 76.2mm light field gun destroyed in the Stalingrad area in late 1942. A German horse-drawn supply column is passing behind the burnt-out STZ-5 artillery tractor and its gun. Nearly 10,000 of the STZ-5s were built and they could tow equipment weighing 8 tonnes or less at 40km/h (25mph). They were much sought after by the Germans.

This captured Soviet position shows a Model 1927 76mm regimental field gun. There are plenty of signs of action, with spent shell cases strewn around. Classified as a small lightweight howitzer, with a crew of three, the Model 1927 had limited use as an anti-tank weapon. Captured equipment was designated 7.7cm Infanteriegeschütz 29(r).

The 76mm M1936 F-22 divisional field gun had a 12ft 6in (3.8m) barrel, no muzzle brake (because it raised too much dust and could compromise its location) a split trail and a crew of six. It could fire fifteen rounds a minute and had a maximum range of around 8.5 miles (14 km). Captured equipment was designated FK 296(r) and later, with many modifications, became the 7.62cm PaK 36(r) anti-tank gun. The weapon was also used on the Marder II and III Panzerjäger.

Above: The Katyusha – Katie in English, a girl whose beloved had gone to war – multiple rocket launcher was nicknamed Stalinorgel (Stalin's organ) by the Germans because the rocket racks looked like organ pipes and when fired, the rockets howled. In service from 1941, it could deliver multiple rockets, fired in sequence, straddle a target area and saturate it more quickly than artillery. It was terrifying for those on the receiving end – at first. After the initial shock came the realisation that it was not accurate. It was slow to load, but quick to disengage – shoot and scoot in today's parlance – before receiving counterbattery fire. The early folding frame held sixteen 42-K rockets that were 1.8m (6ft) long and weighed 42kg (93lb); stability was provided by jacks, as seen in the photo of a partially burnt-out truck and launcher. Usually there were four in a battery, each with a crew of six, supported by two trucks carrying rockets and two technical support trucks. About 10,000 were built during the war. There were many different carrier systems and upgrades.

Opposite above: One of the most heavily produced artillery pieces ever – just over 19,000 variants produced between 1939 and 1960 – the 122mm M1938 (M-30) medium divisional howitzer originally had a fixed-trail carriage and metal wheels, which restricted travel speed. Mass-production started in 1940, with the M-30 now having a split trail and rubber tyres which meant it could be vehicle-towed without a limber (a two-wheeled cart was used to support the trail if pulled by horses). When captured, they were designated 12.2cm sFH 396(r) heavy howitzers.

Opposite below: A knocked-out Soviet 76.2mm M1939 divisional field gun near Stalingrad as photographed by 297. Infanterie-Division. Many of these guns were captured by the Germans in 1941. They rechambered the guns to fire their more powerful PaK 36 ammunition and fitted them with a double-baffle muzzle brake. The resulting weapons were identified by the Germans as 7.62mm Feldkanone 297(r) when used as field artillery and 7.62mm PaK 39(r) in anti-tank service.

# 4 In Defence

AFTER THE YEARS OF attack, the initiative passed to the Red Army in August 1943. After Kursk, the Germans attempted to stay mobile and use counterattacks to stem the enemy's advance, but there were few opportunities to mount major offensives – if only because of their lack of air superiority. Attrition, the need to defend from USAAF and RAF bombing in the west and growing Red Air Force strength and tactical and organisational skills, all these factors disrupted the Luftwaffe's abilities and dispersed its forces. While the VVS could, and did, harry German logistics, supply lines and Luftwaffe airfields, the Luftwaffe in turn was unable to accomplish any major disruption of Soviet forces behind the front lines or supply the intelligence needed for effective defence.

Without functional air support, the Germans struggled to hold a front line after Kursk, and Soviet skills in camouflaging their forces – and their offensive intent – were almost as much of a problem to them as the Soviets' remarkable infiltration skills and the partisan menace in their rear areas. After Kursk, the Germans attempted to set up a defensive line on the Dnieper. Hitler's insistence on *Feste Plätze* and fixed defences certainly did not help the Germans' preferred option of mobile defence, and there is no doubt that German capabilities along the huge length of front were insufficient – especially in the south. Hitler gave approval for the so-called Ostwall (aka the Panther–Wotan Line) on 12 August 1943, at which time the front line was some hundreds of miles to the east. Surely there was plenty of time to build an impregnable barrier? There was not. By the time the southern elements of the Wehrmacht reached it, the Soviet attacks were too strong for them to hold. The southern line gave way, retreated, and by November the Crimea and 17. Armee was cut off. On 9 May 1944 Sevastopol fell.

Elsewhere, between the end of August and the end of December 1943, the Red Army forced the Ostheer back to its Ostwall, regaining huge areas of Ukraine, including Kiev. The Dnieper line was almost immediately pierced by Soviet bridgeheads from which the next offensive saw the southern front line pushed back to the Polish and Romanian borders. In the north, the siege of Leningrad was lifted.

By the end of April 1944, the Germans had just about cobbled together a defensive line but that was blown away by Operation *Bagration* in June–August 1944, ending with German forces along the Vistula in Poland. The second half of 1944 saw Romania, Bulgaria, large parts of Hungary and the Baltic states fall.

German defences were unable to stop the crushing attacks of 1945. Their attempts at holding the Red Army through fixed defensive lines had proved almost as porous as had the Soviets' in 1941 and 1942.

Fixed positions were key to defence in the winter months. In 1941/42, one of the coldest on record, they were essential because defending in the open simply led to frostbite and cold injuries. With no shortage of timber or manpower, Soviet defensive positions were carefully constructed, covered over and offered warmth and protection to the defenders. When the ground was frozen, the Germans quickly learned that grenades or explosives could help. This stoutly constructed bunker shows timber probably topped off with spoil from digging, with natural snow and sheeting to break up the gun slit. Visible inside is a PM1910/30 Maxim MG with armoured shield and crew.

As with all armies, the Germans produced handbooks and pamphlets about field constructions and winter warfare. Bunkers, when they were built, used whatever local materials were available. They were carefully positioned, specific to the weapons they housed and wherever possible were given sufficient covering to cope with bombs and artillery. This bunker's wooden framework may well have been sawn using the acme of petrol-fuelled chainsaws: Stihl's K43 8hp power saw. It had to be used by two men (as all chainsaws were until the postwar invention of swivelling carburettors and floating diaphragms). German strongpoints and fortified defensive positions were linked with communication trenches, MG posts, OPs and road networks. The Soviets' tactical aim was to bypass these by deep flanking moves. This was certainly made easier in the depths of winter when defenders tended to coalesce around villages.

A rather different encampment: this one is for shelter rather than defence. The photograph shows hillside dugouts in a *balka* (ravine) near Stalingrad, probably for the rear echelon, those units that were not needed for direct combat. There are storage dugouts and those for catering or refreshment. A degree of camouflage was provided by the use of *Zeltbahn* shelter quarters.

Above: While trenches conjure up images of the First World War, they were a key part of Second World War warfare too, in particular as protection against artillery, not simply needed in defence. The great *Keil und Kessel* encirclement battles required a constricting ring around the *Kessel* (cauldron), and that meant trenches and foxholes, as here. This front-line two- or three-man slit-trench (*Schützenloch für 2–3 Gewehrschützen*) would have been dug quickly, in two to three hours, as enemy contact was almost inevitable, initially with mortars and artillery.

The Heeres-Dienstvorschrift (Military Regulations) of 1942 stated that these trenches should be dug to a depth of 1.6m or 2m (5 or 6.5ft) with a fire-step and be rectangular, which is not the case here. They offered a degree of protection from direct fire but were intended to be a flexible 'hasty' temporary fighting position. Note the two Kar98k standard-issue rifles, the soldier's lack of webbing and the absence of the black-white-red national tricolour shield on his helmet as it was considered an aiming point for snipers.

Opposite above: In German doctrine the object of defence was to halt an enemy attack, or to gain time pending the development of a more favourable situation for resumption of the offensive. By late 1943, however, defence had become linear with extensive field fortifications, wire and mines; where possible it had a system of mutually supporting strongpoints – and that meant trenches. Basic trench systems had a common layout of three, or more, lines where – as in the First World War – the front line was the fire trench; the second line was the support trench for the front line, housing extra food, ammunition and reserves; the third line held admin, medics, cooks, supplies etc. and the mobile reserve for counterattack.

This photo shows a reserve trench, which could be many miles behind the front line (out of artillery range) but still constructed for defence. The basic trench has been stabilised by using a variety of available construction materials, cut timber (silver birch), what looks like roughly sawn planks or household flooring by the entrance and something metal on the right. Note the soldier's Kar98k rifle in the doorway.

Right: This soldier has compensated for his lack of winter clothing with what is probably a locally made heavy-duty animal-skin overcoat, although it could have come from a Soviet corpse/prisoner or possibly have been sent from Germany after Hitler and Goebbels's plea for winter clothing to be donated to the troops in Russia.

In a frank speech on 20 December 1941, Joseph Goebbels said, 'As long as a single object of winter clothing remains in the Fatherland, it must go to the front … The front needs the following badly, and above all: overshoes, if possible lined ones, or fur-lined ones; warm woollen clothing, socks, stockings, heavy underwear, vests, or pullovers; warm, especially woollen, underclothing, undershirts, chest and lung protectors; any kind of headgear protection, ear muffs, wristlets, ear protectors, woollen helmets; furs in all senses of the word, fur jackets and fur waistcoats, fur boots of every kind, and every size; blankets, especially fur covers, thick warm gloves, again especially fur-lined leather ones, or knitted gloves, and wool mittens; altogether everything of wool is needed urgently on the front and will be doubly welcome.'

The soldier in this photo (right) also has a whitewashed helmet and is wearing sentry winter overboots with wooden soles and felt and leather-strapped uppers.

WL
36923

Above: The best-known German Flak weapon was, of course, the 8.8cm – mainly down to its use in the anti-tank role. Because of its weight, it needed a halftrack prime mover, the mittlerer Zugkraftwagen SdKfz 7, a medium towing vehicle weighing 7 tonnes. This photo shows an 8.8cm being towed through Kremenchuk, south-east of Kiev in Ukraine, in 1942.

Opposite above: Over time, the Red Air Force gained in effectiveness, forcing the Germans into increasing flak protection for both fixed positions and also when on the move. The 2cm Flak 30 Luftwaffe field Flak gun was efficient and reliable but with a slow rate of fire (around 120 rpm from a twenty-round box magazine, just visible on the left side of the weapon; the netting on the other side is to control the ejected cases). It was widely used in a ground role as an anti-tank weapon with its armour-piercing Panzergranate (PzGr) 40.

The gun leader (*Geschützführer*) chose where to site the gun and how to camouflage it. The photo shows it positioned behind a bunker and whitewashed to match the surroundings. The soldier on the right wears a white reversible winter top (trousers as well) over his greatcoat, and a toque, a woollen sleeve that could be pulled over the head to protect the ears and face. The armband, which could also be red, was an essential indication in winter conditions of friend and not foe!

Opposite below: The 2cm Flak 38 replaced the Flak 30 with an improved rate of fire. Entering service in 1940, with the same feed system, lighter and faster to operate, with an improved sight which incorporated a mechanical computing device, it was the most-produced German Flak gun with about 18,000 built. Normally seen on a two-wheeled towed trailer, it was light enough to be manhandled and was man-portable in six loads.

This Flak 38 is on a Luftwaffe Horch 108 (WL numberplate). It is towing a trailer emblazoned with a red star that looks as if it has been cut from one of the four kills identified by rings on the barrel. Note the rolled canvas to the side of the trailer and a mixture of foliage with netting on it and the vehicle. Four of the crew wear the M42 Luftwaffe *Splittermuster* (splinter) camouflage: they are from a Luftwaffe field division. The base colour for the ammo boxes and the fender suggests the vehicle has spent time in hotter climes: certainly, the Horch was used in this form by the Deutsches Afrika Korps.

This set of photographs shows schwere Flak-Abteilung 390(o) – the o = *ortsfest* = fixed position (no organic transport) – of Flak-Division 8 setting up an 8.8cm AA gun position to defend Bremen in north Germany, in 1943. The photos show (above) the gun crew removing the Flak 18 weapon from its Sonderhanger 201 trailer (in an emergency the gun could be fired from its trailer, but in this case the road wheels have been removed and the folding cruciform outriggers are down with screw-jacks adjusted for stability. Note the perforated fixing stake still in the travelling position on the Lafettenkreuz 18 cruciform base). If possible, an 8.8cm would be dug in to reduce its profile but in the second photo (opposite above) protection has been built around it; an open parapet known as a *Bettung* gave the gun an unobstructed field of fire. Muzzle blast would destroy anything, so there would be a 30m (33-yard) clear zone to the front. Note in this and the next photo the turves used to clad the installation and the companion unit in the background.

The final image (opposite below) shows the weapon in its position – note the stake has been inserted inward of the levelling jack. Dora is D in the German phonetic alphabet and probably refers to the gun. The crew numbered eleven: gun commander, halftrack driver, gun layer for elevation, one for traversing, loader, four ammunition handlers, fuse setter and fuse setter/round handler. In these images some are wearing one-piece black *Drillichanzug* (work overalls).

DORA

Opposite above: The 7.5cm PaK 40 anti-tank gun, introduced in 1942, was the principal German anti-tank gun throughout the war and was used as a stand-alone towed weapon (as here) or on self-propelled artillery such as the Marder. (There was also a version used in tank-busting aircraft.) It had a range of ammunition: PzGr 39, an armour-piercing, capped, ballistic cap round; PzGr 40, an armour-piercing, composite rigid round with a sub-calibre tungsten core – the hardness and high density of tungsten made it suitable for penetrating armour but supplies ran out in the later war years; PzGr 38 HL/B, a high-explosive anti-tank round with a shaped (hollow) charge. The photo shows a whitewashed PaK 40 with muzzle cover and a soldier wearing single-piece cotton snow overalls and felt and leather cold-weather boots.

Opposite below: A dug-in 7.5cm PaK 40. This was a scaled up PaK 39, with a double-skinned shield and split tubular trail. With its low profile and a crew prepared to push its stress level – keeping their nerve and letting the target get close – it was lethal. The two helmets and rudimentary cross suggests a soldier has been killed in action.

Below: Maintaining mobility was an important factor in the Germans' ability to hold the Soviets off for so long. They were able to put back into the front line tanks that other countries might have considered write-offs. Mobility was key for the Panzergrenadiers, whose job it was to support the Panzers. 10. Infanterie-Division became Infanterie-Division (mot) in May 1941 and was redesignated 10. Panzergrenadier-Division in June 1943. Like their British counterparts, the Panzergrenadiers were more likely to be transported by lorry than a halftrack (although you would not believe that if you watched wartime film). Keeping the lorries on the road at company level, there was a motor vehicle maintenance section made up of: NCO section leader and master mechanic, NCO mechanic, three mechanics (privates), a driver mechanic, a radio mechanic, a halftrack driver and a driver (all privates). They had a 2-ton cross-country maintenance lorry, a 3-ton cargo lorry for spares and an 8-ton halftrack SdKfz 7 as a recovery vehicle.

Opposite above: The 10.5cm leFH 18 was the standard artillery (howitzer) piece for the Wehrmacht throughout the war but was a bit too heavy to be easily horse-drawn during the winter when a prime mover – the 3-ton SdKfZ 11 or 5-ton SdKfZ 6 – made life easier. To make towing easier, the wooden spoke wheels were replaced with light metal cast wheels with removable tyres. Howitzers are usually indirect-fire weapons (target not seen) but were able to fire line of sight (direct fire), as suggested by the photo. This 168. Infanterie-Division weapon is suitably whitewashed for the conditions.

Opposite below: The main divisional heavy weapon, the sFH 18, was built in large numbers (over 6,750) and was used extensively during the war. It was also adapted for use as an SP gun – the Hummel. Originally designed to be horse-drawn, the gun being separated from the mount, a two-wheel bogie allowed it to be towed in one piece by vehicles such as the SdKfz 7 halftrack – reducing the time it took to ready for combat to three to four minutes. However, it was unsprung, so speeds were limited. It employed a multi-bagged charge system that had to be loaded into a cartridge case; the projectiles being separate.

This photograph shows a sFH 18 battery firing. Note the camouflage netting to hide the gun outlines from recce aircraft. The crew cover their ears. Deafness was a problem, but up to the 1940s it was generally believed that hearing loss could be prevented by developing a tolerance to noise. It would be interesting to know why one of the soldiers is in his underwear. Perhaps a fire order came during ablutions!

Below: Another view of the *'Immergrün'* 15cm sFH 18 howitzer – the family nickname meaning evergreen, enduringly fresh – firing over open sights (or direct fire) at short range where the target can be clearly seen by the layer looking along the barrel. This can and did expose the crew to return fire so was only considered as an emergency method. The photo shows a 16. Panzer-Division weapon, the crew in a mixture of dress, white fatigue trousers and braces over an undershirt and an armless black top. The reality of support arms is that the crew wear whatever is appropriate for the conditions.

The terms of the Treaty of Versailles banned the development of heavy artillery by Germany. One consequence was the development of an alternative: free-flight rockets fired by Nebelwerfer (fog or smoke launcher). When Poland was attacked there were three battalions firing 10.5cm rockets. During 1941, the 15cm Nebelwerfer 41 took over. The six-tube launcher fired rockets spin-stabilised by twenty-six angled exhaust vents for accuracy, with the rocket motor at the front, venturis about halfway down the body and the explosive package in the tail section. Unsurprisingly, accuracy is a misnomer: they were anything but. The rockets were fired from a split-trail two-wheeled carriage in the sequence 1, 4, 6, 2, 3, 5 for stability. They may have been wildly inaccurate individually but when fired with the rest of the battery they caused devastation over a large area. The success of these units led to proliferation and the number of batteries increased, some being motorised using SdKfz 11/4 and /5s as towing vehicles. Later still, there was the Panzerwerfer 42 or 43 on a Maultier (SdKfz 4/1). Larger rockets were also developed, such as the 21cm Nebelwerfer 42, which fired HE rockets from a five-tube unit.

The photo (below) shows a number of Nebelwerfer being fired. 5.5 million 15cm rockets and 6,000 units were produced over the course of the war. Friedrich Sander noted in his diary on 8 August 1941:

'[The] rocket projectiles of the Nebelwerfer battery leave long smoke trails in the sky which usually mark their position clearly. But now the rain is coming down in streams and that seems to be pushing the smoke down again, quite effectively hiding the Nebelwerfer position from the Russian artillery observers on the other side. We, on the other hand, just need to stick to scheduled fire plans.

'At 07.30 the launcher battery fired its first salvo into the morning mist. When the first rocket streaked into the grey sky the first drops had begun to fall and at the time the hundredth round was fired it was already raining quite heavily …

'Damn! I nearly wet myself again, as just now another salvo howled into the sky. There will be several more coming today, I guess. Even though I have now heard this infernal howling and hissing multiple times I seem to be unable to get used to it. It terrifies me every time.'

In 1943 and 1944 the Panzerwaffe was given a more powerful cutting edge by the arrival of new armoured vehicles. Rushed into the fray, these new tanks – Panther, Tiger I and II – were unreliable initially and did not make the entry that was hoped for. Nevertheless, in spite of continued automotive difficulties, they ended the war with fearsome reputations. There were heavyweight Panzerjäger specifically designed to destroy tanks and other armoured vehicles, the heavyweight Ferdinand/Elefant, Nashorn, Jagdpanther and Jagdtiger, and the lighter Jagdpanzer IVs and 38. These photographs show the Jagdpanther, first issued in 1944 and armed with the best German tank gun of the war, the 8.8cm PaK 43/3 L/71 with two-piece barrel and protruding mount. The chassis is based on the standard Panther but with extended upper and sides, a single vision slot for the driver next to the gun mount and an MG 34 on the other side. The remaining crew had periscopes on the top. Close protection was provided by a Nahverteidigungsgerät (close-defence weapon). The lack of turret allowed more ammunition storage, better crew conditions, thicker armour and was cheaper to produce. Note the *dunkelgelb* paint scheme.

The artillery also received improved SP guns in 1943 in the form of the Grille, Wespe, Hummel and Sturmpanzer (or Brummbär = Grouch). The Hummel (Bumblebee) mounted a 15cm sFH 18 L/30 heavy howitzer on a PzKpfw IV chassis (schwere Panzerhaubitze auf Geschutzwagen III/IV Sf). Introduced in May 1943 as artillery support for armoured units, like the Panther and Ferdinand, it first saw action at Kursk in summer 1943. It fought in batteries of six with a dedicated ammunition carrier also on a PzKpfw IV chassis. The Hummel had a crew of six (commander, driver, radio operator and three gun crew) but could only carry eighteen rounds of HE. Note the canvas top-cover to keep the weather out and the heat in; it had cabin heating from the engine during the Russian winter, and an anti-grenade wire cage. MG 34s and 42s gave close-quarter defence. The soldiers beside the vehicle are three Germans and a Hungarian officer at right.

## Life in the Line

An important part of life in the line was hygiene – something less easy to maintain in the advance. There are three parts of the body that must be kept clean: teeth, bottom and genitals and feet. If any of these areas became infected, the soldier becomes a burden to others. He has to be taken out of the line and requires treatment that should have been avoidable. Shaving the scalp was the only way – other than using chemicals – to avoid the relentless itching and scratching of lice. In cramped unsanitary conditions lice flourished; where there was hair, there were lice. They were carriers of bacteria which could impact on soldiers' lives, health, morale, stress and combat effectiveness. Lice also spread typhus.

Preparing for battle. It could come at any moment, so it was important to ensure that the rounds were fitted correctly into the continuous link belt to prevent stoppages. A long and tedious task, it was undertaken by everyone when an opportunity arose – in this instance a nice clear blue sky. Note that he has covered his back to keep the sun off it – it was a chargeable offence to get sunburn – and to stop the belted rounds from burning him.

Luftwaffe personnel around an open fire. The two despatch riders, one sitting, the other standing, wear olive-green rubberised full-length coats made by the French company Ariel Moulins for the Wehrmacht in the 1940s. The airman standing on the left has the NCO's silver braid around his collar and epaulettes. He wears two awards on his chest; the Iron Cross 1st Class and another, possibly a Qualified Air Gunner Badge

If an opportunity arose to freshen up and get clean it was taken. Bathing raises everyone's spirits and morale and gives a good chance to lark around – the Germans also have a word for it: *herumalbern*, behave in a silly way.

This doctor's tent is made up of a number of triangular *Zeltbahnen* linked together by cord and pegged down. The camouflage is splinter and each side was a lighter or darker version. The mapcase would hold pencils/crayons and sharpener in the outer leather tubes along with a pouched ruler. The contents would be appropriate to him and the map.

When it's cold, there's nothing better for morale than hot food. The daily ration was supposed to provide an average of about 4,500 calories a day: a cold portion (bread, fat, sausage – fresh or in cans – or tinned fish or cheese, marmalade or artificial honey, seven cigarettes or two cigars), a warm portion (potatoes or partially substituted with vegetables – fresh or dried – bread or pastry or rice, fresh meat, salt and spices, bean coffee and ersatz coffee or tea), and other items depending on availability, such as eggs, fruit, chocolate etc.
On the front line rations were delivered at night in large *Essenträger* carried as a backpack. Carrier troops were sent to the rear to collect these along with mail. Here, hot food is dished out of an *Essenträger* into mess tins.

Opposite: A Luftwaffe Gefreiter (airman first class/lance corporal) with red collar tabs indicating that he is in a Flak unit eats from the standard cooking pot/mess tin (Kochgeschirr 31) which had a capacity of 1.71 litres (3 pints). Looks cheesy!

Above: A quiet spell allows the crew of an SdKfz 251 halftrack a personal hygiene moment as an Obergefreiter (senior lance corporal; he has less than six years' service as there is no pip on the arm badge) cuts a crewmate's hair. Tarpaulins partially cover the open top to form a shelter, but also to break up its silhouette from the air. The small white ball on a stick behind the man at right allows the driver to maintain a distance from the kerb when driving by keeping the ball in line with it. The K indicates that the vehicle is part of Panzergruppe 1 (K = *Kleist*) of Heeresgruppe Süd.

Opposite: If the opportunity arose, the German Army bought fresh food rather than stole it – but only in areas where they felt a kinship – Denmark and Norway, for example – and with an exchange rate that favoured the Reichsmark. As far as the east was concerned, there was a plan; a cold-blooded heartless plan proposed by SS-Obergruppenführer Herbert Backe that intended to remedy the German deficiencies in home production of food by seizing it from the Russians and giving it to their soldiers and citizens instead. They accepted that this would lead to famine and the death of millions. The effects can be seen in the deliberate starvation of Soviet PoWs that contributed to the death of so many of them. In pro-German areas of Belarus and Ukraine some markets like this existed and there would be payment of a sort. The overall plan stuttered, in part thanks to Soviet tactics. As they retreated during Operation *Barbarossa* they used scorched-earth tactics: they left absolutely nothing behind and what they could not take they destroyed. Sander's diary entry of 31 July 1941 makes it clear he was not aware of the Backe Plan:

'Besides we have noticed that the collectives and kolkhozes are either hiding all their cattle or they are driving them to the north, away from us. That puts us at quite a disadvantage, as that means that, in addition to petrol and ammunition, our supply units also have to drag huge amounts of food across enormous distances. But in general there is nothing to complain about. There is enough bread and crispbread and that is quite filling. We just have to be careful with what we have and take the rest from the land if we can find something. If only the potatoes were ready to harvest. Now the thoughtless infantrymen dig whole potato fields over just to find enough to fill one small basket with potatoes. And in the winter it is we who can feed the population. And we already have the whole of Europe hanging on our shirt tails.'

Peeling spuds, a task familiar to most soldiers. This happy-looking bunch – would they rather be changing wheels like those behind them? – appear to have a Hiwi amongst them (looking at the camera). He wears the Soviet *pilotka* universal cap and what looks like the M43 *gimnasterka* pull-over blouse which came down to mid-hip level and was made from cotton rather than wool. Fresh food was rare in attack. Friedrich Sander recorded in his diary on 15 July 1941:

'In the meantime I have eaten something. Two sandwiches with cheese and one with blood sausage. And it's not even Sunday. Anything but blood sausage is usually reserved for Sundays. Otherwise the tinned stuff … is the pillar of our daily meals. Blood sausage in tins, liquified from the heat of the tank, is usually served in the mornings and evenings while lunch often consists of pea, lentil or bean soup. That in turn has the effect that the air in our tents during the nights is a lot warmer. And it also seems to aid the Landsers' digestion, woe to those who dare to go deeper than 15 metres into the woods alongside our routes of advance and get lost in a maze of paper and fly-covered little piles. One can easily find the advancing army. Just follow the smell.'

Cooks from II./63. Artillerie-Regiment prepare a meal. Note the Morris Commercial CS8 in the background. Many of these sturdy vehicles were captured at Dunkirk, Crete and the African desert and saw German service through to the end of the war. They were modified to carry light guns, or were used as prime movers, recce vehicles and load carriers. The man at left is using a portable haversack water filter. Issued on a company basis, it could process 100–250 litres (22–55 gallons) of water per hour, depending on the amount of solid matter in suspension.

Above: A 'homely' environment was good for morale; just getting away from it all. It was important for the family at home to know by letter that their boys were being looked after, but tablecloth and flowers were a bonus. The reverse was also true, especially after the bombing started. Soldiers needed to know that their families were safe and were receiving the food and/or loot parcels. There was a degree of censorship, but not with the rigidity of the Allies. In the background a pair of Gulaschkanonen (mobile field kitchens) and a horse-drawn Red Cross wagon can be seen. The canvas to the right looks like British 'Mickey Mouse' pattern vehicle canvas – quite possible because of the many British vehicles captured in France.

Opposite: Darning socks in the field is not as easy as it might look. The secret is to keep the repair smooth, otherwise there is a risk of blisters. Usually, a darning mushroom was used – as its name suggests, a smooth wooden aid, looking like a mushroom. In this photo an M24 Stielhandgranate (stick hand grenade) is being used as a substitute. Note the sock-size white bands, the camouflaged M43 *Feldmütze* side cap and the paraphernalia on the other side.

This SdKfz 221 has been camouflaged and its outline broken up by the use of vertically placed wood. The crew has set up a machine gun in the wall, and one of the two (the 221 had commander and driver) is taking the opportunity to write a letter home. As mentioned earlier (see p. 132) the SdKfz 221 was the Wehrmacht's original light armoured car. With a two-man crew it had a turret mounting an MG34 – some were later armed

with a 2.8cm sPzB 41 anti-tank rifle – on a standard four-wheeled heavy passenger car. This one – seen in the Crimea in 1942 – is identified (by the symbol on its rear left plating) as belonging to a Kraftradschützen (motorcycle) unit.

*Heimaturlaub* – the opportunity to go home on leave – depended on circumstance, location and availability of transport, amongst other potential barriers. There was leave to visit family or get away from the front lines, but length and frequency were often limited and as the war progressed opportunities to take leave diminished. Those who did manage to get home had strict instructions to be positive about their experiences and not demoralise those at home by being negative. It was important for both parties to reassure each other that everything was fine and not to worry.

For those not visiting family there was an opportunity to relax, perhaps in the *Soldatenheime* where they could relax, have a decent meal, shower, catch up with the news, have alcohol, buy luxuries such as fresh fruit and confectionary. In some locations there would be the chance to replace worn-out uniforms and some kit, and visit dental and medical facilities – a few days to escape the harsh realities of war. Friedrich Sander wrote:

'This morning I was with the baggage, which is not far away. The tailor and the shoemaker were also at work there, so I took the opportunity to have my trousers repaired which were quite spectacularly torn. I also accessed my suitcase, depositing several maps of our advance route in it. The key I keep in the document case, which is stored on Oberfeldwebel Oswald's lorry together with the captured material, but I managed to open it by trying a few other keys. I wonder when I will ever be wearing the clothing inside it again.'

A moment's peace in the sunshine, and the opportunity to study a map. The Germans had pretty good maps, although they had a lot of catching up to do after the restrictions imposed on them at Versailles. When the Nazis came to power, they restarted the programme. In 1936 Oberst Gerlach Hemmerich became head of the new 9. Abteilung, Generalstab des Heeres (Army Surveying and Military Geography of the Army General Staff). In 1939 it was reorganised into the Abteilung für Kriegskarten und Vermessungswesen (Directorate for War Maps and Surveying). In 1941, Hemmerich was promoted Generalleutnant and became Chef, Kriegskarten- und Vermessungswesen (Head, Military Maps and Surveying). From 1942, a new Deutsche Heereskarte (German Army Maps) standard appeared with military grids and updates using the latest aerial photography and, where possible, field checks (for more detail see article by Susan Powell and Heiko Mühr).

This photo was taken from inside a café, which accounts for the ghost images. The accordion is being played by an Oberschütze (senior rifleman). Horner was probably the largest manufacturer of accordions in the world but in the mid-1930s the accordion was associated with jazz, decadent in the eyes of the Nazis. Horner cleverly pushed the blame onto the saxophone and said that the accordion was perfect for German folk music. The subterfuge worked and on the outbreak of war Horner was able to advertise: 'The rifle is the bride

of the soldier, but the accordion his girlfriend.' Thousands were distributed to the military to boost morale and prevent boredom during the long periods of inactivity – accounting for the many photos of them being played by soldiers on the Eastern Front. Coincidentally, the Red Army too had a penchant for the accordion.

The children's faces show a mixture of emotions.

Music was an escape from reality. Most units had a musical instrument and someone who could play it – an accordion or harmonica, for example – to lift the spirits or help deal with the stress and trauma of combat. Others might have a record player, as seen in the photo.

The 16. Panzer-Division Obergefreiter has a white band on his epaulette signifying an aspiring officer (Offizieranwater) – and what better time to crank it up and listen to music than when involved in a monotonous job. Cleaning weapons was important but boringly repetitive. Here the man on the right is about to wipe down a Kar98k rifle and the man in the centre a handgun, probably a Soviet TT-33 Tokarev semiautomatic pistol. The latter is wearing an Iron Cross 1st Class pinned to his chest and the ribbon for an Iron Cross 2nd Class by the buttonholes (this cross was worn on presentation only). There's a lot of kit lying around, including an ammunition box that probably holds the communal cleaning bits and pieces.

The Nazis had a difficult relationship with the Church and religion. Germany was a Christian nation and Hitler could not be overtly antithetical at first – there are strong signs that he expected to eradicate all religions in the long term. In the short term, the Nazis needed to keep the religious elements of the nation onside because most of their support came from rural and small-town Protestants. Nevertheless, much of their rhetoric was against the Church. There were chaplains in the German Army – the usual figure given is around a thousand – and there is no doubt they played an important role, particularly as the casualties mounted. The Nazis promoted the *Heldentod* (hero's death) – and a staple term of praise printed on the *Sterbebilder* or death cards sent out in memory of fallen soldiers was *Ich gab mein Leben in Gottes Hand und starb als Held fürs Vaterland* (I gave my life into God's hands and died a hero for the Fatherland).

Hitler was introduced to the Catholic faith by his devoutly religious mother but drifted away after leaving home. It is believed that he remained a Christian but never attended church. However, he feared the political influence of the Church, feeling that it might undermine his agenda, so on 20 July 1933 he agreed the Reichskonkordat with the Vatican that guaranteed the Catholic Church's rights but banned it and its representatives from participating in politics. Most soldiers were Christian: after all, their belt-buckle was stamped *Gott mit uns*, God is with us! They valued church services, to some extent – particularly after they started helping the Einsatztruppen – to salve their consciences and during the early days field communion was a regular occurrence.

Soldiers remember their dead. They respect their dead. The dead provide an incentive for action. If at all possible, dead soldiers were given a hand-painted wooden cross and a Christian burial: here (above) a marker for the grave of Gefreiter Schweigt of 10./Infanterie-Regiment 212.

Soldiers' graves were treated with great reverence, were tended and adorned with flowers. This photograph (right) shows a soldier serving with Panzer-Artillerie-Regiment 75 of 3. Panzer-Division at a graveside. It is taken in front of the Anastasia Chapel in Hlukhiv, Ukraine, in 1942.

## Portrait of the German Soldier

It is very difficult to categorise the German soldiers on the Eastern Front because they changed so much during the war. Nevertheless, it is true to say that their enemies respected them as fighting men while deploring their involvement in all the vile aspects of the Nazi regime. That they – from the most senior Generalfeldmarschall to the lowliest *Landser* – were heavily involved in atrocities and genocide is incontrovertible: whether many of them had a realistic opportunity to behave differently is more debatable. The Wehrmacht and the Nazis were quite happy to execute their own for anything from bad-mouthing the Führer to desertion.

The German Army of 1941 – successful in war, believing in its cause, with high morale and excellent training – was better armed, better led and better organised than any other of the time, certainly than the Red Army. Motivation is a significant factor for military forces, and the German Army was extremely well motivated thanks to the massive anti-Soviet propaganda campaign that the Nazis promoted, at its heart the fact that communism, Jews and Slavs needed to be wiped from the map in order to provide peace and the living space Germans required.

Reading the letters and diaries of German soldiers reveals that the commitment to this cause was very real in the early years and helped motivate the soldiers to plough on into Russia as their comrades fell beside them. After the realisation came – for most at some time in 1942 – that the Soviets were unlikely to be defeated quickly, if at all, disillusion and despair set in. But there was rarely a change in political views. And as far as defeatism went, by the time the army was in retreat, the soldiers clung to two beliefs: that the Führer and his secret weapons would come to their rescue, and that they had to keep the Red Army from doing to their families and homeland what they had done to the Soviets in 1941 and 1942. When the Red Army started entering German territory proper, with its lavish houses and high standard of living, their reaction was as uncompromisingly hostile as the Germans expected. Unsurprisingly, in the latter stages of the war the German armed forces spent much of their time fighting towards the west in order to be captured by the British and Americans rather than the Soviets.

By the end of the war, the Wehrmacht had changed markedly from the all-powerful force of 1941. First and foremost, it had fewer allies. Often treated with contempt, the Italians – save for some of the Fascist National Republican Army – had left in March 1943; the Romanians in August 1944. The Hungarians tried to leave in 1944 but the Germans occupied the country in March 1944 and stopped them. By June 1944 the small number of Slovak forces fighting for the Nazis had been turned into construction workers.

What the Wehrmacht had gained were Waffen-SS units recruited from European countries such as Spain, the Netherlands and Scandinavia. Then there were the Osttruppen – some 800,000 men, many impressed into service but also many who wanted to fight against communism and for their own nationalistic reasons. There were also the Luftwaffe Field Divisions (not to be confused with the Fallschirmjäger units which were proved time and again to be elite and professional, as were the Flak gunners with their 8.8cm weapons, the best anti-tank gun of the war). The wrong men for the job, poorly trained in land warfare, the Luftwaffe units had to be transferred to army control in late 1943 and ended the war being used for rear-echelon duties as far as possible.

This is what a Luftwaffe Generalmajor wears when the weather is cold. Erich von Falkenhayn began his military career during the First World War as a fighter ace and is credited with twenty-six victories. He served under the Nazis until 1942. He wears the standard blue-grey gaberdine wool overcoat with silk-like lining, white piped collar and gold pebbled buttons. The belt has a double-claw pebbled buckle. The sheepskin greatcoat was reversible and had a large collar in a contrasting colour. Some were made to a set pattern at factories in Germany or in occupied territories. Others were made locally by the unit tailors (or local) in the theatre of operations but not necessarily to the standard pattern. Many had tuck-away cotton hoods. He wears an issue toque under his scarf, around and over his head. His headwear, difficult to see clearly, might be the blue-grey officers' replacement flightcap (*Einheitsfliegermütze*).

General der Panzertruppe Hans-Valentin Hube led 16. Panzer-Division in Heeresgruppe Süd and would go on to command the German forces in Sicily. He is seen in Russia wearing a black woollen wraparound Panzer field jacket. His *Waffenfarbe* is pink (*rosa*), as are the *Totenkopf* collar patches and staff officer's (Stabsoffizier) ornate pattern shoulderboards with battalion number. Other than the *Totenkopf* collar patches, *Waffenfarbe* piping was discontinued mid-1942. On his head is the old-style *Feldmütze* with no cap cords.

Generaloberst Heinrich von Vietinghoff commanded XXXXVI. Armeekorps (mot) until June 1942, when he became deputy commander-in-chief of 9. Armee. In this early summer 1942 photograph he appears to be wearing a waterproof motorbike coat. His car, a Kfz21 Horch 901/40 cabriolet 1941, has a framed general's pennant with a field-grey cloth base trimmed with gold bullion wire *Tresse*, swastikas on the bumper and an Armeekommando plate above the numberplate.

Generalleutnant Erich Hoffmann looks rather pensive. An Austrian who joined the Wehrmacht after the Anschluss in 1938, he started the war as Chief of Operations of XVIII. Armeekorps but by 1943 led 207. Sicherungs-Division, part of the Rückwärtiges Heeresgebiet Nord. He wears the M36 field-grey double-breasted overcoat with red wool lapels and dark-green collar, gold pebbled buttons and double-clawed pebble buckle. He has an Iron Cross 2nd Class ribbon on a buttonhole.

Generalfeldmarschall Günther von Kluge meets Generaloberst Heinrich von Vietinghoff in late 1941. Kluge commanded 4. Armee during Operation *Barbarossa* and replaced Fedor von Bock as commander of Heeresgruppe Mitte in December 1941. He was badly injured in a car crash in 1943 and was replaced by Generalfeldmarschall Ernst Busch. Kluge is seen holding his Generalfeldmarschall's interim baton (*Interimstab*) for everyday use rather than the heavily jewelled and valuable primary baton (*Marschallstab*) used for ceremonial occasions. Only eighteen such army batons were awarded.

Generaloberst Heinz Guderian in front of his Horch Kfz 21 staff car (note the Panzergruppe symbol on wheel arch above the bumper) while on a visit to 3. Panzer-Division. Panzergruppe *Guderian* became Panzergruppe 2 in November 1940 in time for *Barbarossa*. In November 1941 it changed again to become 2. Panzerarmee. Guderian did not keep his position for long after this, dismissed by Hitler after his army was dislodged from its positions around Moscow.

Both the Wehrmacht and Waffen-SS had units of special forces, the former being the Brandenburg Division; the latter, Sonderlehrgang zbV *Oranienburg* (zbV = zur besonderen Verwendung = for special duties), changed its name various times and, from 1943, was headed by Otto Skorzeny. While Skorzeny achieved fame for taking the limelight during the rescue of Mussolini (the operation was, in fact, mainly undertaken by Fallschirmjäger), the Brandenburgers proved more effective spearheading the German invasions in west and east, advancing clandestinely into enemy territory ahead of the armoured columns to take key bridges or

transport nodes. Here, Brandenburgers are about to leave by train for Ukraine in 1942. Note the lack of national emblem on their tunics. One of the Brandenburg units advanced further into the Caucasus than any other Germans. In September 1944 the Brandenburg Division became a line infantry division – although some 1,800 men transferred to Skorzeny's Waffen-SS unit. Panzergrenadier-Division *Brandenburg* was destroyed in fighting at Memel and Pillau on the Baltic.

Left: Josef Heindl was commanding I./Infanterie-Regiment 199 *List* of 57. Infanterie-Division as Hauptmann der Reserve (Captain of Reserves) when he won his Knight's Cross of the Iron Cross (*Ritterkreuz des Eisernen Kreuzes*), for his skilful defence near Sumy in Ukraine. He received the award on 9 February 1943 and on 18 November received the Oak Leaves (*Eichenlaub*) to the Knight's Cross, but it was posthumous; he fell in the front line. He is sporting his Knight's Cross in this photo, along with the Iron Cross 1st Class on his breast pocket (awarded 3 June 1940; the 2nd Class was won on 9 October 1939), below which are the Infantry Assault Badge in bronze (he also received the silver posthumously) and Wound Badge in silver (2nd Class), representing three or four wounds. On his right breast he wears the German Cross (*Deutsches Kreuz*) in gold, awarded on 26 December 1941.

Above: Two infantry Oberfeldwebel (sergeant majors) – note the M40 shoulder-boards with silver *Tresse* and pips – and a staff officer seen in 1942. Note the difference in footwear: the NCOs are wearing *Marschstiefel* (marching boots), which were gradually phased out as the war progressed. The officer wears *Schnurschuhe* – lace-up shoes – universal wear by the middle of the war. He also has *Gamaschen* (puttees) because he is wearing breeches which end just below the knee. Each has the Iron Cross 1st Class on the left chest pocket. Other decorations include the Iron Cross 2nd Class medal ribbon and silver Infantry Assault Badge (left); black Wound Badge (centre) and Infantry Assault Badge (right).

An odd couple photographed in summer 1941 by Heinz Eckert of Propaganda-Kompanie 670: at left an Unteroffizier holding a magazine-less MP 38 has both a camera and a version of the M25 map case with an aluminium-tipped strap and housing. Note the lip or resting bar under the barrel to keep the weapon steady when firing through a port or over the edge of the vehicle. He is talking to a Gebirgsjäger officer (note the Edelweiss badge on the side of his *Bergmütze* – mountain cap). They are leaning against a Soviet truck.

After the medal ceremony, twelve proud recipients of the Iron Cross 2nd Class – awarded for an act of bravery in the face of the enemy – pose for the camera. There is a mixture of units, ranks and uniforms. Two wear the M36 tunic (*Waffenrock*) with the dark blue-green collar, the others the early version of the M43 without the dark blue-green collar but still with pleated, soon to go, pockets. The two officers (at right) have breeches and longer boots. On the extreme right the cavalry officer wears spurs and a lightweight white cotton summer uniform top. The officer next to him has the two-claw brown officer's belt and wears an old version *Feldmütze* 'crusher style' – with the inner cap spring removed. Interestingly, none have any other award on their chests.

Is it beginning to get colder? Some of this infantry unit have been able to appropriate Red Army *ushanka* headwear. Most wear the M38 or M42 *Feldmütze* side cap and a number have the Infantry Assault Badge on the left breast. They are carrying their Kar98k rifles and have slung their helmets until the shooting starts again.

The walking stick has been a feature in European culture for centuries, but these are special.

The *Wolchow* stick is named after the Volkhov river near Leningrad (with German transliteration), where between 1941 and 1943 Heeresgruppe Nord fought in an area of forest and bog they dubbed the 'arse of the world'; the men were 'bog soldiers'. Many of these sticks were made by the wounded for commanders, NCOs and officers, as a token of respect; a reminder of the awful conditions all lived under. Each stick is unique, recording the circumstances that warranted it, and were held in high regard by those presented with one. This group of 212. Infanterie-Division officers show off a disparity of uniform colours and two finely carved sticks.

In the early days, the Germans struggled with warfare in Arctic conditions. Recognising that the Finns were masters of winter warfare, they persuaded them to supply instructors. By winter of 1941/42 officers and senior NCOs were withdrawn from the Eastern Front to attend these intensive courses, skiing included. These Gebirgsjäger are training with 160cm skis and ski boots.

Gefreiter Hugo Krause wears the *Bergmütze* with a white metal Edelweiss flower with stem and a small standing chamois emblem beside it – that of 5. Gebirgsjäger-Division. His M36 jacket had specially cut sleeve ends that allowed it to be rolled tightly and buttoned for ease of putting on gloves.

With a backdrop of Norwegian mountains, a Flak Oberleutnant sits astride a bench showing off his Crimea Shield (*Krimschild*), M43 *Einheitsfliegermütze* cap and 1937 second model *Offizierdolch* (dagger) with *Portepee* (sword knot). The Crimea Shield was created in 1942 after the fall of Sevastopol and was awarded to Wehrmacht forces who had fought in the Crimea between September 1941 and July 1942.

Opposite: This Luftwaffe Hauptmann sports an Iron Cross 2nd Class ribbon and a set of medal ribbons (L–R): First World War Iron Cross 2nd Class, Honour Cross of the World War 1914/1918 with Swords (denoting a front-line veteran) and Prussian General Medal of Honor 2nd Class. Note the particular version of the national eagle insignia (*Hoheitsabzeichen*), its eagle's wings beating – unlike those of the army.

German paratroopers used camouflage jump smocks from 1941, the Luftwaffe *Splittermuster* 41 was the first. This (opposite) Obergefreiter (leading aircraftsman) was photographed in 1941 wearing a parachute smock – *Knochensäck* (bone bag) – over his uniform. On his breast he wears a *Fallschirmschützenabzeichen* (Parachutist Badge) for having completed six jumps. By 1944, Fallschirmjäger were no longer making parachute jumps and were being used as elite ground troops. Their clothing (above) was camouflaged jacket, Luftwaffe *Einheitsfeldmütze* cap and service dress trousers. The Fallschirmjäger fought with great intensity on the Eastern Front, and – as elsewhere – always punched above their weight.

The SS used a range of camouflage patterns (*Muster* = pattern): *Platanenmuster*/plane tree (1937–43), *Rauchtarnmuster*/smoke camouflage (1939–44), *Palmenmuster*/palm (1940–43), *Eichenlaubmuster*/oak leaf (1941–45), the captured Italian *Telo mimetico*/camouflaged tarpaulin (1943–45), *Erbsenmuster*/pea (1944–45) and right at the end of the war *Leibermuster*/body (1945). This one (right) is *Erbsenmuster*.

Above: The early war *Schutzmütze* had a rounded inner crash liner that made the beret look too big for the wearer. This Panzer radio operator is buttoned up in a standard-issue field-grey army greatcoat with dark blue-green collar and black shoulder straps with pink edging. The greatcoat proved unwieldy and cumbersome in a tank and was soon discarded in preference of the heavier reversible winter clothing.

Opposite: A tank driver at rest, reading a magazine. He wears a *Feldmütze* and sits next to a jerrycan. The driver was recognised as being a key element in the crew, and where they could, the others cut the driver some slack, picking up some of the minor chores to allow him to rest.

Above: Medals are important to army personnel. They show others that the recipient has walked the walk. Friedrich Sander received his Iron Cross 1st Class (EK1) in the field: 'After a Feldwebel of 6th Company has been decorated with the EK1, he [Oberstleutnant Alfred Siebert, company commander] flips the paper he is holding over and reads: "Leutnant Sander". Then he rummages around in the other trouser pocket and pulls out a little paper bag. I am angry about all this! Even Father Christmas brings his presents in Mother's potato sack and not in his trouser pocket. And for this kind of benediction I have risked my life … Anyway, now I have visible proof that I am not a coward.' This 22. Panzer-Division Iron Cross award ceremony is taking place at Kherson in 1942.

Opposite: The *Panzersonderbekleidung*, the iconic black uniform worn by the Panzer divisions, had pink piping around the collar and distinctive *Totenkopf* collar patches until 1942, as shown by this Gefreiter, who is holding his *Feldmütze* under his left arm. The uniform was noticeable, as Friedrich Sander remembered in his diary entry of 25 October 1941: '[We] cheated our way past the 12-kilometre-long column of vehicles queuing up on the bridge. I had taken off my coat and stood on the footboard in my black uniform and with all gongs well visible. I had the pistol in my trouser pocket and the handle of the 08 was sticking out … no one dared to stop me and let me pass, even if it took a lot of shouting and cursing.'

Above: Grimy with dust from the dirt roads, their uniforms faded from the summer's heat, these medical officers of 9. Panzer-Division look as if they have made hard yards in the early days of *Barbarossa*. 9. Panzer was part of Panzergruppe 1 in Heeresgruppe Süd until late September when, during the fighting at Briansk, it became part of Panzergruppe 2 in Heeresgruppe Mitte. At left an Oberstabartz (Major); right, an Oberarzt (Oberleutnant). It is hard to tell from this photograph, but their *Waffenfarben* are cornflower blue (*Kornblumen blau*) and each has a golden snake and staff motif.

Opposite: Signals Oberleutnant (note *zitronengelb* – lemon yellow – *Waffenfarbe*) of Panzer-Nachrichten-Abteilung 27 of 17. Panzer-Division away from the front in 1944. He is wearing an M43 *Einheitsfeldmütze*, not to be confused with the earlier *Bergmütze*, which had a shorter peak.

The staff of 3./Artillerie-Regiment 157 – the third battery in I. Abteilung of 57. Infanterie-Division's artillery regiment – show off their field service uniforms (note the fading on the seat reinforcements of the breeches), bright red (*hochrot*) *Waffenfarbe* and medals. The three on the left have the Iron Cross 2nd Class ribbons in their second tunic buttonholes and two of them sport the 1st Class award on their breast pockets. The Oberleutnant at right looks to have the War Merit Cross. The infantry division's organic artillery regiment had one 15cm howitzer and three 10.5 howitzer or gun battalions, each with a staff and three batteries of four guns to give forty-eight in total. Later in the war this was reduced to thirty-six by losing twelve of the 10.5s. The staff of a battery would comprise the chief, the battery troop leader, a VB (forward observer) officer and an observation officer in charge of the survey unit: so, four officers (as here), along with thirty NCOs and 137 other ranks. Most often the weapons were horse-drawn, as were the ammunition and communications wagons, and supply/commissary/pack trains. In total there was a complement of 153 horses in the official reckoning.

The Reichsarbeitsdienst prepared young men for service in the armed forces. After war was declared, RAD units were transferred straight into the army's Bautruppen – construction troops. By 1942, many young RAD-*Männer* (such as this one) were serving in the Soviet Union – over 400 RAD units – and many of them ended up fighting. Towards the end of the war, a number of RAD infantry units were formed, although only three saw significant action.

Unlike the SS, the Wehrmacht used fewer forms of camouflage clothing. The first and main one was developed in the early 1930s but dates back to the First World War: *Splittermuster* 31/splinter pattern, which was in use 1932–45. The Luftwaffe produced its version, Luftwaffe *Splittermuster* 41 (used 1941–45) – see pp. 252–253 – and the German Army developed *Sumpfmuster* 43/swamp, in use 1943–45; then *Sumpfmuster* 44, in use 1944–45 (information from Michael Farnworth). This Horch 108 Type 40 (external spare tyres dropped) driver wears *Splittermuster* 31 camouflage trousers, a reversible winter jacket (mouse-grey side out) and a rather smart fur hat.

This Leutnant (note the rank insignia on his left arm: it was used on camouflage or special combat clothing) from 12. Infanterie-Division is wearing a reversible winter uniform that was introduced in winter 1942/43. Double-breasted for extra warmth, large enough to be worn over the field uniform and equipment (although most wore the equipment on the outside), it had a separate hood with drawstrings – as here.

14. Panzerjäger-Kompanie of 6. Infanterie-Division show off their winter clothing near Rzhev in 1942. Each infantry regiment had infantry gun (13.) and Panzerjäger (14.) companies and the Panzerjäger were usually motorised. In the early war period they typically used a Kfz 69 (such as the Protze) to carry crew and ammunition (thirty-six anti-tank and twenty-four high-explosive shells) while pulling the gun, a 37mm

PaK 35/36. The guns changed during the war, although 42mm/50mm and 75mm weapons were slow to reach all units. This meant many of the Panzerjäger units ended up in close combat with the enemy's tanks, using such weapons as Molotov cocktails until the Panzerfaust came in around 1943 and gave tank-hunters a reliable short-range weapon. The Panzerjäger *Waffenfarbe* was *rosa* (pink).

By 1943 the Germans had sorted out its supplies of winter clothing, as these photos show. Some – usually sentries or officers – were lucky enough to get hold of sheepskin or fur coats, many of which were picked up or altered locally. Major Scheer (above) of 207. Sicherungs-Division – part of Rückwärtiges Heeresgebiet Nord, the command that handled the Army Group North Rear Area – employs a white cloth to camouflage his helmet and is wearing a sheepskin coat very similar to the Swedish *Livpäls* M/1913 which was used by Finnish troops. 207. Sicherungs-Division was created from 207. Infanterie-Division and spent most of its existence in Estonia before it was disbanded in 1944.

# 5 The End

By the time the Red Army stepped across the Oder–Niesse line on 16 April 1945, it had wiped out German resistance in most areas – with the heavily defended Courland pocket the only notable exception in the east. Between them and Berlin were the German defences on the Seelow Heights that had been carefully prepared by Generaloberst Gotthard Heinrici. Within a few days the Soviet forces had crushed the opposition, encircled 9. Armee in the Halbe pocket, advanced west to stop Wenck's 12. Armee from becoming involved in the battle for Berlin and, on 25 April, completed the encirclement of the German capital.

The Germans had lost the war; all they could do now was postpone the final rites. They did so until 2 May, by which time some 200,000 German soldiers and civilians were dead. Over 500,000 had been taken prisoner.

With the political framework of postwar Europe in mind, Stalin rushed his forces west and south-west. Budapest had fallen on 13 February, Vienna by 13 April. Unconditional surrender had taken place on 8 May, but the fighting took a little while to finish. Between 6 and 11 May the Red Army took Prague. The final fighting in Czechoslovakia was on 11 May. On 13 May, the Red Army stopped all offensives in Europe and accepted the surrender.

On 1 August 1945 the Potsdam Agreement, signed by the United Kingdom, the United States and the Soviet Union, agreed the military occupation and borders of Germany.

## The Cost

The war in the east killed millions, either directly or indirectly through disease, starvation and the byproducts of war. The precise figures are difficult to identify and there is much argument about them. However, what is clear is that, as well as through fighting, the German Army and occupation forces murdered millions of civilians (estimates are between 14 and 17 million) – mainly, but in no way limited to, Jews and Poles. About 6 million Poles died during the German occupation in the war, half of them Jews. That figure increases by around 100,000 with the inclusion of those killed by the Soviets.

The military losses are dwarfed by the civilian casualties but were still huge.

Opposite: Winter 1944/45 saw Hitler squander any opportunity the Germans had to maintain a defensive wall in east and west by using up new equipment and divisions in the Battle of the Bulge. German losses were high, many of the losses caused by crew abandonment after running out of fuel. This Panther looks unharmed, has engine hatches open and towrope unstowed, so it probably ran out of fuel and was left for dead. Note the camo scheme and the extra armoured 'chin' on the mantlet which identifies a late Ausf G.

**Axis Powers military losses in the East (all figures estimated)**

| *Country* | *PoWs* | *PoWs died in captivity* | *Total military dead* |
|---|---|---|---|
| Germany | 3,000,000 | 500,000 | 4,000,000 |
| Soviet Hiwis/etc | 400,000 | c.200,000 | 215,000 |
| Romania | 500,000 | 55,000 | 281,000 |
| Hungary | 500,000 | 55,000 | 300,000 |
| Italy | 70,000 | 27,000 | 82,000 |
| Finland | 3,500 | 500 | 63,000 |
| Total | 4,500,000 | 850,000 | 5,000,000 |

**Soviet Union military losses (all figures estimated)**

| *Country* | *PoWs* | *PoWs died in captivity* | *Total military dead* |
|---|---|---|---|
| Soviet Union | 5,700,000 | 3,300,000 | up to 10,000,000 |
| Poland | Unknown | Unknown | 24,000 |
| Romania | 80,000 | Unknown | 17,000 |
| Bulgaria | Unknown | Unknown | 10,000 |
| Total | up to 5,750,000 | 3,300,000 | 10,000,000 |

Note: Total military dead includes PoWs died in captivity/missing presumed dead/suicides/executed

The Plattensee Offensive around Lake Balaton in March 1945 was one of the last major operations by the Panzerwaffe in the war. Initial successes were stopped by the Soviet forces, whose counterattack pushed the Germans back into Austria. A month later Vienna was in the hands of the Red Army. This photograph shows a StuG III Ausf G undergoing repairs at the time of the offensive (note the open engine hatches). In the foreground are IF-8 trailers – a box with a tubular framework that could be manhandled or towed by horses and was often connected to other IF-8s – for example, when transporting the 8cm mortar and its ammunition. They were not intended to be towed by vehicles. Covered in camouflaged *Zeltbahnen*, visible on the right are two Feldfu b1 radio transceivers (one on the top, one against the wheel) and three of the Panzerfaust hand-held anti-tank weapons that proved so effective in the last months of the war.

Horses one way, trucks the other – German supplies and Romanian infantry retreat before the Soviet attacks in 1944. The Romanians resisted until 23 August 1944, when King Michael I led a coup and changed sides, declaring war on Germany that night. The resulting armistice signed on 12 September saw over half a million men of the Romanian Army forced to fight against their one-time allies: they sustained 167,000 casualties by war's end.

Romanian soldiers retreating in good order. The Romanians had proved themselves in the fighting at Odessa and in the amphibious operation that took Novorossiysk and were unfairly scapegoated as the reason for the encirclement of 6. Armee at Stalingrad. It is true that they were crushed by the Soviet attack but they had been tasked with defending a long front line without sufficient support or heavy weapons. Operation *Uranus* ravaged the Romanian Third Army, which eventually broke and ran after being outflanked, allowing around 300,000 men – including Romanians – to be encircled in the city.

Above: The German equivalent of the British 'Dad's Army', the Home Guard, was the Volkssturm – all men aged from 16 to 60 who were not already serving. They were ordered to take up arms to defend the Fatherland and their local communities. Announced to the public on 16 October 1944, the resulting force was undertrained, ill-armed and often ineffectual. Some units fought hard – particularly in the *Festungen* of the Eastern Front and in the Battle of Berlin – but many melted away when they neared action. It was a desperate act by a desperate regime. This shows Volkssturmmänner in a Berlin barracks in 1944.

Below: 11. Panzer-Division did not enter the war until it took part in the invasion of Yugoslavia, but was involved in hard fighting after that at Moscow, Kiev, Voronezh and in the battles along the Chir river. It fought at Kursk and then was involved in the defensive battles in the Donets and then Kharkov regions, and by the end of May 1944 was in the foothills of the Carpathians. Sent to southern France to recuperate, the division was once again forced to retreat, this time by the landings on the French Riviera. It fought in the Saar, at Remagen and ended up in Neumarkt, Czechoslovakia, where it surrendered to the US Third Army. Here, PzKpfw IVs of the division head towards their surrender. The Ausf J in the lead shows well the three-colour camouflage of the late war, with *dunkelgelb* as the main colour and secondary colours of *rotbraun* and *olivgrün*.

The crew of an M8 Greyhound of 121st Combat Reconnaissance Squadron, US Seventh Army, surrounded by German soldiers marching into captivity. 121st Cavalry rescued King Leopold of Belgium from his prison in Strobl, Austria – a spectacular end to a war that had taken them from Normandy to Austria by way of Alsace and the Saar. They would go on to be part of the occupying forces in Austria until October 1945.

Luftwaffe personnel march towards confinement. They all seem to be well provisioned and the cleanliness of their uniforms speaks of their lack of fighting. Note the two Gefreitern with *Tätigkeitsabzeichen* (trade/specialty badges): at left, the crossed muskets indicates *Waffenpersonal* (armourer); at right, the winged badge is for *Flugzeugpersonal* (technical aircraft personnel).

Looking for souvenirs after Waffen-SS officers surrendered their pistols to the 101st Cavalry Regiment in Schwendt, Austria. The photograph was taken by Colonel Leslie Crozier Wood, who was in one of three jeeps that was part of the group who took the surrender of SS-Gruppenführer und Generalleutnant der Waffen-SS Max Simon, who was later convicted of war crimes, particularly while commanding 16. SS-Panzergrenadier-Division Reichsführer-SS.

SS-Obersturmbannführer Albert Ekkehard was Max Simon's chief of staff while he commanded 16. SS-Panzergrenadier-Division and later when he took over SS XIII Armeekorps. In this photo, also taken by Leslie Crozier Wood, Ekkehard is at left seen talking to an American army translator from 101st Cavalry Regiment in Schwendt. Next to Ekkehard is a Waffen-SS officer wearing a Sturmgeschütz grey-green jacket.

## Berlin

Nothing, perhaps, sums up the war better than the destruction of Berlin. The Wehrmacht had failed to take Moscow but the Red Army was not going to falter. The battle was bloody; estimates vary, but around 80,000 Red Army and up to 100,000 German soldiers died. The civilian losses were huge: some 125,000 and those that survived had to endure a savage occupation. Four years after *Barbarossa* began, the Red Army – fuelled by a hatred exacerbated by what they had seen in their own country as they retook it – took a ghastly revenge on the population: looting, rape, murder and starvation ensued. Today, we can point to many factors that contributed and, unlike the Nazis, Soviet commanders did regain control of their troops and made efforts to feed the German citizens, over a million of whom were homeless.

These photos show Berlin in 1946, well after the battle and after the clearup and rebuilding process had started. This period was the start of another postwar trope, the *Trümmerfrau* – the cheerful 'rubble women' who helped clear the debris all over Germany. While it is true that – particularly in East Germany – women were 'encouraged' to take part, few in the west did so with the alacrity later politicians suggested, in spite of the incentives (such as improved ration cards) dangled in front of them. Today, however, the myth endures in numerous statues.

Above: The Kaiser Wilhelm Memorial Church, the famous 'hollow tooth' of Berlin, was built by order of Kaiser Wilhelm II in the late 1890s. Badly damaged, it was not rebuilt after the war but left as a memorial.

Below: Looking down today's Strasse des 17. Juni (the old Charlottenburger Chaussee, which was renamed to remember the 1953 uprising in East Berlin) past the Soviet War Memorial (note the pair of T-34s at left) towards the Brandenburg Gate. The war memorial at the Tiergarten was unveiled in November 1945.

Above: A StuG III Ausf G, missing its gun barrel, rusts away in the Tiergarten. In the background are the white statues on Neues Siegesallee. Originally standing on Siegesallee between Königsplatz (today's Republic Square), where the Victory Column stood, and Kemperplatz, the statues – thirty-two marble monuments showing the key political players of Brandenburg and Prussia between 1157 and 1888 – were created between 1895 and 1901 on the commission of Kaiser Wilhelm II. Speer's grand plans for Hitler's rebuilding of Berlin saw them moved to Grosse Sternallee, which was renamed Neues Siegesallee. It was opened to celebrate Hitler's fiftieth birthday on 20 April 1939. The Soviets built their war memorial on the original Siegesallee, which only exists today as a walking path.

An American soldier sits on a dug-in PzKpfw IV. On 22 February 1945, 5. Panzer-Kompanie (bo) Berlin – where bo = *bodenständig* = static – was set up to defend key locations in the city. The company received ten Panthers and twelve PzKpfw IVs that were too damaged to be returned to the front. Without engines, they had crews of three (commander, gunner, loader) and came in two forms: the turrets alone inserted on a casemate and the engineless vehicles dug in. Most were sited at important road junctions, and this one is identified as being in the Tiergarten.

The remarkable Hochbunker Pallasstrasse, the building the US Army tried to destroy in postwar years, is still there today. Built by forced Soviet labour between 1943 and 1945, it was destined to be used by the Reichspost (German Postal Service). The Allied bombing campaign put a halt to that. It is a stark reminder of the past.

A burnt-out T-34/85 in the Tiergarten. Note the remains of the white band around the turret – an air recognition symbol. The Soviets lost at least 2,000 tanks in the Berlin offensive.

The Neue Reichskanzlei – Albert Speer's extension of the Chancellery, built between 1934 and 1943 – housed Adolf Hitler's grand office and a series of enormous rooms, including this one, the Mosaiksaal (Mosaic Room).

The Führerbunker beneath the old Reich Chancellery was where Hitler spent most of his last days. This is the garden entrance (door in grey central building). The two towers are ventilation and guard towers, the left-hand one still under construction. Between them, closer to the right-hand one, was the pit in which the bodies of Hitler and Eva Braun were burnt.

# Sources and Further Reading


## Printed Books

Archer, Lee & Nevenkin, Kamen. *Panzerwrecks 20 Ostfront 3*. Panzerwrecks, 2016.

Beiersdorf, Horst. *German Military Trailers and Towed Equipment*. Schiffer, 1995.

Beiersdorf, Horst. *Bridgebuilding Equipment of the Wehrmacht*. Schiffer, 1998.

Brooke, Andrew. *Air War Over Russia*. Ian Allan, 2003.

Buchner, Alex. *The German Infantry Handbook 1939–1945*. Schiffer, 1991.

Buchner, Alex. *The German Army Medical Corps in World War II*. Schiffer, 1999.

Chamberlain, Peter & Doyle, Hilary L. *Encyclopedia of German Tanks of World War II*. Arms & Armour Press, 1978.

Chew, Allen F. *Leavenworth Papers No 5: Fighting the Russians in Winter: Three Case Studies*. Combat Studies Institute, 1981.

Cooper, Matthew. *The German Army 1939–45*. Macdonald and Jane's Publishers, 1979.

Coox, Alvin D. & Naisawald, L. van Loan, *Survey of Allied Tank Casualties in World War II*. Johns Hopkins University Press/Dept of the Army, 1951.

Dallin, Alexander. *German Rule in Russia 1941–45*. Macmillan, 1957.

Davis, Brian L. *German Army Uniforms and Insignia 1933–1945*. Brockhampton Press, 1998.

Davis, Brian L. *Uniforms and Insignia of the Luftwaffe* (2 vols). Arms & Armour Press, 1999.

Frank, Reinhard. *German Heavy Half-Tracked Prime Movers*. Schiffer, 1996.

*The German Campaign in Russia: Planning and Operations (1940–1942)*, Department of the Army Pamphlet 20-261a. 1955.

Glantz, David M. & House, Jonathan M. *When Titans Clashed: How the Red Army Stopped Hitler*. University Press of Kansas, 2015.

Hitler, Adolf. *Mein Kampf.* Translated into English by James Murphy, a Project Gutenberg of Australia book.

Hogg, Ian V. *German Artillery of World War II*. Greenhill, 2002.

Jentz, Thomas L. (ed.). *Panzertruppen*, vols 1 and 2. Schiffer, 1996.

Kopenhagen, Wilfried. *German Infantry Carts, Army Field Wagons, Army Sleds 1900–1945*. Schiffer, 2000.

Krivosheev, Grigori F. & Kruglov, Aleksandr. *Soviet Casualties and Combat Losses in the Twentieth Century*. Greenhill, 1997.

Liedtke, Gregory. *Enduring the Whirlwind: The German Army and the Russo-German War 1941–1943*, Wolverhampton Military Studies Book 21. Helion, 2016.

Mayer-Stein, Hans-Georg. *The Medium PKW of the German Wehrmacht 1937–1945*. Schiffer, 1998.

Müller-Hillebrand, Burkhart H. *German Armored Traffic Control During the Russian Campaign*; Department of the Army Pamphlet 20-242. June 1952.

Müller-Hillebrand, Burkhart H. *German Tank Maintenance in World War II*, German Report Series. Department of the Army, 1954.

Nafziger, George F. *The German Order of Battle Panzers and Artillery in World War II*. Greenhill, 1999.

Overy, R.J. *Why the Allies Won*. Jonathan Cape, 1995.

Sander, Friedrich. *Blood, Dust and Snow: Diaries of a Panzer Commander in Germany and on the Eastern Front 1938–1943*. Greenhill, 2022.

*Soviet Field Artillery in the Offensive*. US War Department, Military Intelligence Division, 1945.

Westerlund, Lars. *The Finnish SS-Volunteers and Atrocities 1941–1943*. Finnish Literature Society, National Archives of Finland, 2019.

Zaloga, Steven J. & Ness, Leland S. *Red Army Handbook 1939–1945*; Sutton Publishing, 1998.

**Articles and Online Sources**

Davie, H.G.W. 'The Influence of Railways on Military Operations in the Russo-German War 1941–1945', *Journal of Slavic Military Studies*, Vol. 30, Issue 2, 27 April 2017.

Ehrenhain Zeithain, 'Wehrmacht and Prisoners of War', Zeithain Memorial Grove website, https://en.stsg.de/cms/node/928#:~:text=A%20circular%20for%20camp%20guards, among%20Soviet%20prisoners%20of%20war.

Farnworth, Michael. 'Introduction to German World War 2 Patterns', Artizan Designs website, https://www.artizandesigns.com/guides/germanpatterns.pdf.

Goebbels, Joseph. 'Plea for Clothing for German Troops on the Russian Front', 20 December 1941. Accessed via the Jewish Virtual Library, https://www.jewishvirtual-library.org/joseph-goebbels-plea-for-clothing-for-troops-on-the-russian-front-and-hitler-s-proclamation.

Halder, Franz. *War Journal* (7 vols). Accessed via the Ike Skelton Combined Arms Research Library Digital Library, https://cgsc.contentdm.oclc.org.

Khromeychuk, Oleysa. 'Ukrainians in German Armed Forces During the Second World War', *History*, Vol. 100, No. 5, December 2015, doi 10.1111/1468-229X.12129. Accessed via https://ueaeprints.uea.ac.uk.

Maubach, Franka, 'Siegen Helfen', *Zeit Online*, 24 May 2011. Accessed via https://www.zeit.de/zeit-geschichte/2011/02/Frauen-im-Ostfeldzug/komplettansicht.

Nafziger, George F. '19th Panzer Division 28 June 1942', the Nafziger Collection of Orders of Battle. Accessed via the Ike Skelton Combined Arms Research Library Digital Library, https://cgsc.contentdm.oclc.org/digital/collection/p15040coll6/id/1357/.

Nuremberg Tribunal. 'Judgement: Keitel', Nuremberg Trial Proceedings vol. 1. Accessed via Yale Law School Avalon Project, https://avalon.law.yale.edu/imt/judkeite.asp.

Powell, Susan & Mühr, Heiko. 'Capturing the Complex Histories of German World War II Captured Maps', *Journal of Map and Geography Libraries*, Vol. 16, No. 2, 2020.

Renner, Stephen. 'The Hungarian Air Service, 1918–45', DPhil thesis, University of Oxford, 2014. Accessed via https://ora.ox.ac.uk/objects/uuid:e0bc090c-41fc-413c-bbe2-37aa06b90dbe/files/m730d33dff693062c787a33286cc99997.

Romaniuk, Scott Nicholas: 'Becoming Hitler's Army: Nazi Killers and the Making of Genocidal Warfare', *Terra Sebvs*, Vol. 2, 2011. Accessed via https://www.academia.edu/72865177/Becoming_Hitlers_Army_Nazi_Killers_and_the_Making_of_Genocidal_Warfare?rhid=28465367819&swp=rr-rw-wc-27691837.

US War Department. 'A Critical Analysis of German Operational Intelligence, Part II', in Military Intelligence Division report, 'German Operational Intelligence', Washington, DC, 1946. Accessed via https://www.nsa.gov/portals/75/documents/news-features/declassified-documents/cryptologic-spectrum/critica_analysis_ii.pdf.